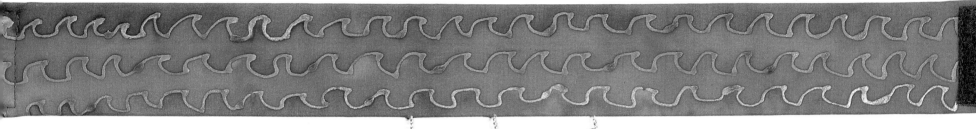

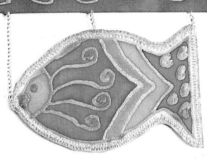

THE STEP BY STEP ART OF

Making Jewelry

This edition published in 1995 by Whitecap Books Ltd
1086 West 3rd Street, North Vancouver, B.C.
Canada V7P 3JS
CLB 4091
© 1995 CLB Publishing Ltd,
Godalming, Surrey, England

Printed and bound in Singapore

ISBN 1-55110-227-7

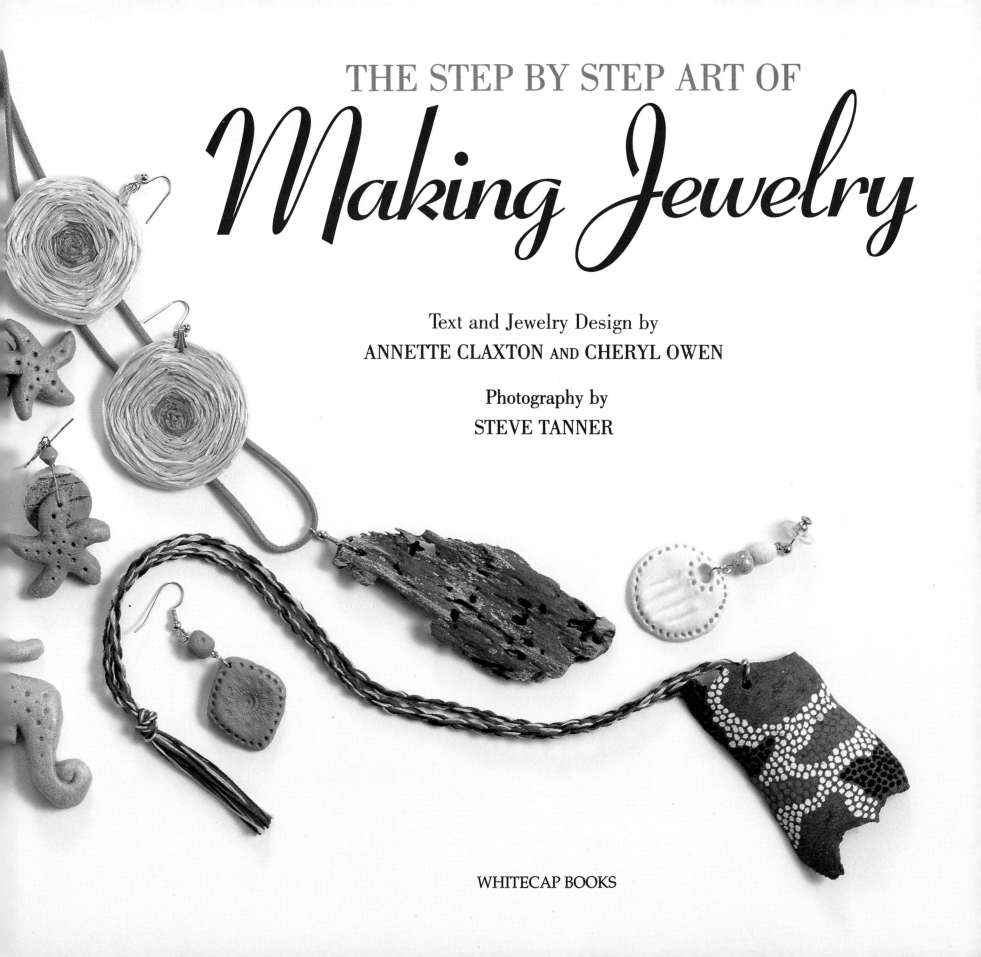

THE STEP BY STEP ART OF
Making Jewelry

Text and Jewelry Design by
ANNETTE CLAXTON AND **CHERYL OWEN**

Photography by
STEVE TANNER

WHITECAP BOOKS

Contents

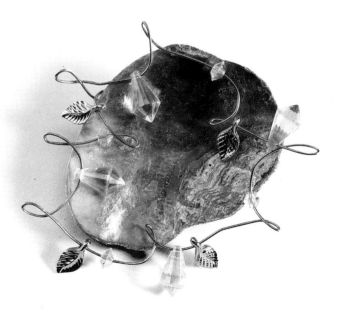

Equipment

There are surprisingly few essential tools needed to make the vast range of jewellery in this book. For comfort and safety work on a clean, flat surface that is well lit and keep sharp implements and glues out of a child's reach.

Cutting and modelling tools

Pliers are vital for most jewellery-making procedures. If you only have one pair, snipe-nosed pliers are the most versatile as they will make wire loops and squash wire crimps closed. Round nosed pliers are used to make loops in wire and flat nosed pliers for squashing closed crimps.

Ideally, use wire cutters to cut wire although a pair of old scissors will suffice for fine wires. Use sharp scissors to cut threads, fabric, leather and paper. An old pair of scissors can be used to cut thin metal. File the edges of cut metal with a metal file. Cut card and mounting board with a craft knife. Always use a craft knife on a cutting mat and replace the blades regularly. Do not press too hard or attempt to cut right through thick card on the first approach; gradually cut deeper and deeper. Cut straight lines against a metal rule. Model papier mâché pulp, clay and salt dough by hand or with clay modelling tools which are available from art and craft stores. A small knife is useful for cutting the modelling materials. Clay and salt dough can be rolled out flat with a rolling pin.

Use a hacksaw to saw wood. Wooden, papier mâché, clay and salt dough modelled jewellery can be sanded with fine sandpaper.

Adhesives

The large variety of materials that can be made into jewellery means that more than one adhesive may be needed to stick a particular item. Always follow the glue manufacturer's instructions carefully and test first on scraps of your materials.

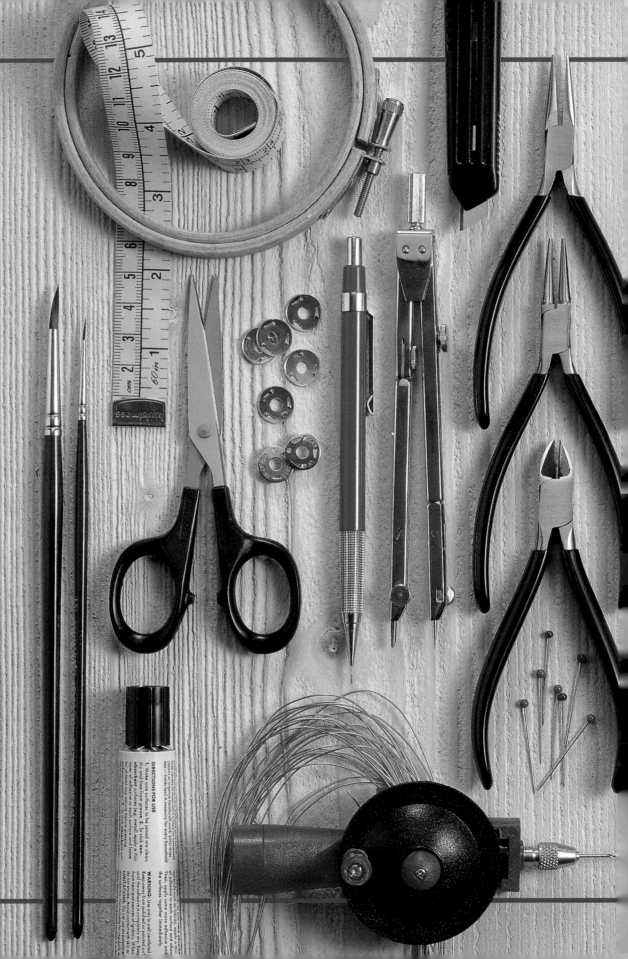

Super glue (strong epoxy resin) is very strong and will stick metals, wood, card, paper, fabric and some plastics. Always handle super glue carefully. A gel glue is easier to apply when only a small amount is required. A dab of super glue helps to secure thread knots. Always store it upright to prevent clogging. All purpose household glue is useful for sticking card, leather and fabric. Stick modelling clay with a glue recommended by the clay manufacturer.

PVA (Poly Vinyl Acetate) medium, available at art and craft stores, is a non-toxic adhesive that dries to a clear, glossy finish. A solution of PVA medium thinned with water is used to make papier mâché. It can also be used as a varnish.

Masking tape can be used to hold smaller pieces in position, while you are working on them.

Pins and needles

Tiny beads should be threaded with a beading needle which is very long and fine. If you find the length difficult to handle, use a size 10 embroidery needle instead. Alternatively, make your own needle by bending fine fuse wire in half then twisting the ends together forming a needle.

Fabric jewellery will require more sewing equipment, pins, needles and threads. Embroidery rings are useful, especially for holding pieces of silk for silk painting, or for machine work. A knitting needle is useful for prodding the jewellery, and a tape measure for measuring wrists and necks.

Holes can be made in various ways depending upon the materials used. A thick needle, awl or compass point can be used on fabrics, thin plastics and metals, leather and card. A craft hand drill or electric drill with a fine drill bit is needed for harder materials such as thicker plastics and metals, wood and shells.

Paintbrushes

A range of paintbrushes will be needed if you intend to make your own beads. Good quality artist's paint brushes are worth the expense. Use a fine paintbrush for detailed work. Always clean brushes thoroughly immediately after use.

Findings

Some of the findings used to make your jewellery may be found in general stores, but for a more comprehensive range visit a specialist bead shop or jewellery-making supplier, many of which have a mail order service.

For pierced ears, there are earring wires (A). Components can be glued to flat pad ear studs (B) or hung on earstuds (C) which usually have a small ball with a loop underneath to hang your decoration from. Secure stud type earrings to the ear with a scroll or 'butterfly'.

For unpierced ears, there are clip-on earring backs (D) which can be glued on, or earclips and earscrews (E) to hang decorations from.

Headpins (F) are similar to dressmaking pins but much larger. Beads are threaded on, then a loop is made at the top of the wire for hanging. Headpins can also be used to make triangular finding shapes and large jumprings.

Necklace clasps come in a variety of styles from simple boltrings (G) and torpedos (H) to lavish clasps (I). Choose a fastening to suit the design of your necklace.

Fix the threaded beads to the clasps with calotte crimps (J) which are two small hinged cups with a loop attached. The knotted thread ends are enclosed between the cups and the loop fixed to the clasp. Endclamps (K) are fixed to the end of cord. A boltring fastening is then attached.

Jumprings (L) are rings available in different sizes that join components together. Choose a jumpring suitable for the size and weight of the pieces to be joined. If you do not have a suitable jumpring, make your own. Split rings are like tiny keyrings and can be used for the same purpose.

Pendant holders (M) are also known as bails. They have prongs to hold your decoration. Bell caps (N) sit over knots on necklaces or earrings.

Other findings include ring backs (O), cuff links (P), brooch backs (Q), hat pins, stick pins and necklets.

Frames of several shapes (R) can be purchased for mounting embroidery and silk designs. They are simple to close at the back with a backing plate.

Materials

Much of the fun of jewellery-making is working with the endless choice of materials that can be used. Beads from all over the world are increasingly available, not only in specialist bead shops, but in craft stores and haberdashery departments in large stores.

Unexpected sources also provide materials to make into exotic designer-style accessories. Browse around your local do-it-yourself store, stationers or motor accessory shop. Use your imagination to think up new ways of using the products on sale and looking at the shop displays with new eyes will soon become second nature.

The minimal cost of most components is an added advantage. And you will soon find many recyclable materials in your own home.

Ready-made beads

Glass, ceramic, wood, plastic and metal are just a few of the materials from which beads are made. The cost of beads varies enormously, but just one or two expensive, choice beads on a necklace can be displayed to great effect amongst smaller inexpensive beads or spacers. Spacers are simple beads positioned between the main beads; they will prevent a necklace looking too heavy and can add a touch of colour or sparkle if they are of a different colour or style to the other beads.

Small glass or plastic rocaille and bugle beads which are used in embroidery are available in a huge colour range. Just a few beads or sequins can uplift a design.

Semi-precious jewellery stones or cheaper varieties made of glass or plastic come in many colours or shapes. Some have holes drilled so they can be sewn or attached with jewellery findings. Glue undrilled stones in place. Some stones are faceted and therefore will catch the light when they are worn.

Sequin dust is made from the holes pressed from sequins. They add sparkle when glued to jewellery.

Keep beads and other components in containers where they will be free from dust. When working with beads keep in saucers where they will be easy to select. Arrange beads for a necklace on a towel so that they do not roll away. A white or skin toned towel is best as a strong coloured towel will affect the appearance of your design, and the colour of the beads you are working with.

Clay and salt dough

Make high quality beads inexpensively from clay. Air drying clay is available from art and craft shops. Keep unused clay in an airtight container. Any spare clay that you are working with can be covered with a damp cloth. When you have modelled the clay set it aside to harden – remember to pierce any holes needed. The hardened clay can be painted although the natural or terracotta colouring of the clay is very attractive. Varnish the pieces for protection. Coloured plastic clay that hardens in the oven (available from art, craft and toy stores) is highly versatile. It is hardwearing and comes in a rainbow of colours. Hot water plastic is another alternative, and is great fun to work with.

Glass jewellery stones and broken fragments of mirrors and ceramic tiles can be embedded in the clay which is then baked for a short time in a domestic oven. Knead two colours together to make a new colour or to create a marbled effect.

Salt dough modelling is an exciting craft medium. Flour, salt and water are kneaded together to make a pliable dough that can be modelled easily. Food colouring can be added to the dough to colour it. The model is then baked hard in a cool oven. Salt dough must be varnished and kept away from moisture.

Paper and card

Perhaps the most readily available materials for jewellery-making, paper and card can be transformed into stunning accessories. Paint offcuts of mounting board or tear newspaper into strips to

make papier mâché. Even waxed paper fruit cartons can be cut up to make quick, fun styles. Model papier mâché pulp (available from art and craft shops) into dramatic shapes and emboss the surface with buttons or a knife tip. Papier mâché applied in layers is surprisingly hardwearing. Giftwrap and textured papers can be applied as a final layer to the papier mâché. All papier mâché components should be kept away from water.

Stick foil papers and sweet papers to large beads to give them sparkle. Tissue paper, although delicate gives interesting effects when coloured layers are overlapped.

Threads

The most common threads for stringing beads are nylon or cotton thread, nylon line (fishing line) or tiger tail (plastic coated wire). Silk or linen thread, cord and plastic, cotton or leather thongs and lengths of ribbon are other possibilities. Cord can be made using a sewing machine. Use nylon or cotton thread threaded on a needle for small and lightweight beads. Cotton thread is the most versatile as nylon thread is prone to wear and tear if threaded through sharp edged holes in beads.

Nylon line and tiger tail do not need a needle to thread them through beads and are suited to larger, heavier beads. Large holed beads can be threaded onto fine chain, cord or thonging. Stiffen cord ends with nail varnish or adhesive-tape to thread them easily. To quickly make a necklace or bracelet, thread lightweight beads onto elastic thread. Knot the thread ends together and adjust the knot to hide it in a bead hole.

Keep a tape measure close at hand when making bracelets and necklaces. As a guide, the average bracelet length is 18cm (7in), although this varies depending on the size of your wrist. A loose choker necklace is 40cm (16in) long, a short necklace is 45cm (18in) long and a long length necklace is 65cm (26in) long. It is not necessary for a necklace longer than 60 cm (24in) to have a fastening that needs to open and close; simply fasten the ends with a reef knot. Adjust the knot to hide it in a bead.

Metals and plastics

Thin copper and other metal sheets are available from craft shops and can be folded into exciting three-dimensional forms. Use printed metal drink cans to make into jewellery too.

Experiment by scrunching aluminium baking foil into bead shapes or covering a plastic bangle with foil. The foil can then be painted or left in its shiny metal state.

Cut coloured plastic bottles into simple shapes to thread up for bracelets and necklaces. Cut plastic drinking straws into short slices to quickly make interesting beads.

Plastic tubing, foam and acetate film can also be made into pieces of jewellery.

Make plastic curtain rings into bold dangling earrings and paint or cover plastic bangles to transform them into stylish designs.

Natural materials

The soft porous nature of balsa wood and drift wood means that they are ideal for turning into jewellery components. The wood can be painted, stained or simply varnished. Matchsticks and lolly sticks are other possibilities to be made into attractive jewellery pieces.

Pierce a hole in melon or pumpkin seeds to make quirky beads. Pretty shells make delightful holiday accessories. Raffia is great fun to work with and the coloured varieties provide lots of design scope.

Try partnering twigs and feathers for an interesting brooch.

Fabrics

Silk and cotton fabric can be used for making patchwork, either glued or sewn.

Gloving leather and suede are soft and easy to work into imaginative designs, and felt is another interesting idea. As an additional advantage, neither felt nor leather will fray.

Stiff interfacing is another non-fraying material, which has been used creatively throughout the book, because it is so easy to sew, glue and paint.

Machine embroidery uses a rich variety of threads with glossy and sparkling effects, and has the advantage of being light to wear. Vanishing fabric is easy to use as a base for solid stitch items, like the crocodile earrings see page 96.

Cross stitch can be worked on linen, Aida or plastic canvas, using tiny beads to highlight the designs worked.

Iron-on transfer paper can be bought in good haberdashers or sewing suppliers. This is used to transfer motifs onto the fabric.

Unusual materials such as upholstery cord and macaroni, bulldog clips and DIY nuts and bolts can all be used in jewellery making.

Paints and varnishes

Craft paints are ideal for painting many of the projects in this book. The colours mix easily, give good coverage and dry quickly. Most are non toxic and are available in gloss, matt, pearlized and metallic finishes.

Indian inks give a translucent effect and work well on papier mâché pulp and salt dough.

Spray paints are easy to use and give good coverage. The metallic colours are highly suited to jewellery making. Always use a spray booth to spray paint. Spray in a well-ventilated room and protect the surrounding area with newspaper. Please use sprays that are free from CFCs.

Glitter paints are available in bottles and tubes. The glitter is suspended in a gel-form adhesive which hardens when dried.

Gouache paint gives a matt finish and always needs to be varnished, but it is easy to use. The paint is water-washable too.

Felt-tipped pens are good for colouring in woods and papers.

Many handcrafted beads and components will need to be varnished. Choose a varnish to suit the material or paint finish. Polyurethane varnish, available in gloss, satin and matt finishes, is hard wearing although it does have a yellowing effect.

Water based varnishes are quick drying and dry to a clear finish. As the items to be varnished are not large, a specialist varnishing brush is not necessary; a paintbrush will suffice.

Wire

Bonsai wire is a thick pliable wire sold at garden centres. It is easy to bend into different shapes for pendants and earrings.

Colourful plastic covered electricity wire can be used in the same way. Paper clips also come in a range of colours and stripes.

Specialist bead shops and jewellery making suppliers sell wire for making into jewellery findings. The wire can be bought in various thicknesses, and is available in gilt, copper, surgical steel, silver plated and gilt plated varieties. The most versatile wire thickness is 0.5mm (^{1}/4in) but finer wire can be used for beads with tiny holes. A thicker wire such as 1mm (^{1}/20in) is suited to heavier beads.

Techniques

As jewellery-making involves using smallish items, beads and earring wires which can sometimes be difficult to use there are a few techniques which are very useful. The methods used to hold smaller pieces of fabric and beads while working with them make the craft much more accessible, and the tips for fixing jumprings are important. Before making any item read all the instructions thoroughly, and follw only the metric or imperial measurements. All the techniques described here have been used throughout the book.

Free machine embroidery

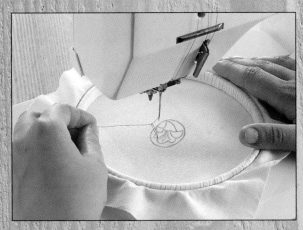

To adjust the machine: remove straight stitch foot, lower feed dog or cover it with tape. Set the stitch length to zero and to the desired width. Frame fabric, place under needle and lower foot lever. Hold top thread and bring bobbin thread to the surface. With needle in the fabric, hold both threads and secure with three stitches. Now sew randomly.

Using a template

Templates for many projects appear on page 98-107. Trace the template onto tracing paper, mark details then cut out. Either use the paper template or make a sturdier version with card. Now trace the template on your material on the wrong side. Use a knife to 'draw' on clay or dough. Use double-sided tape to stick the template to fabric or wood.

Sewing on cold water soluble fabric

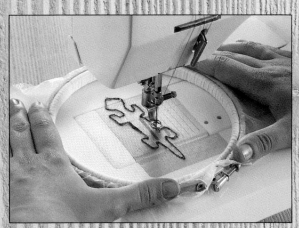

1 Place soluble fabric into the frame, making sure it is taut. Position the frame over your design and trace the design using marker pen. Sew around the outline with two rows of straight stitching; either one on top of the other or with a second row close to the first. Then set the machine to zig-zag stitch and sew over the outline to strengthen the edges.

Painting beads

For ease of handling when painting, decorating or varnishing beads, insert a cocktail stick into the bead hole. If the hole is too large, pad out the end of the cocktail stick with a little cling film (plastic wrap). Insert the cocktail stick into plastic clay or polystyrene until the bead has dried.

2 Continue random stitching, ensuring that the stitches are well integrated, building up texture and linking the centre to the edges as the fabric will dissolve later. Soluble fabric may shred if it is stitched heavily, but more pieces can be added to strengthen areas.

Making a rouleau tube

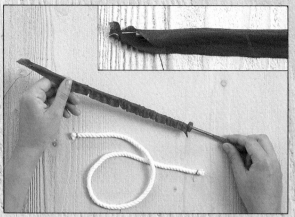

1 *Find the true bias of the fabric by folding a square of fabric diagonally, so that the cut edge is level with the selvedge edge. This fold will stretch well. Mark along this fold either with a ruler or with a steam iron. Measure the width required for the rouleau and rule a second parallel line.*

2 *Cut out the fabric. Sew together along the long edge taking a narrow seam allowance, and using a polyester thread for strength. Turn through to right side using a special tube turn wire or by attaching a safety pin to the end threads and pushing the pin back through the rouleau.*

Sewing on stiff interfacing and canvas

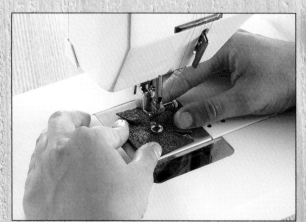

3 *Loosen the tension if threads break, although this may also be due to the type of thread you are using. Once sewing is finished, cut away excess fabric and immerse in cold water until all the fabric has disappeared. Pat with a clean cloth to remove surface moisture and lay out to dry.*

These fabrics do not require framing and can be freely machined. The designs can either be drawn onto the fabric or cut out when the embroidery is finished. The fabric edges can also be painted.

Painting on silk

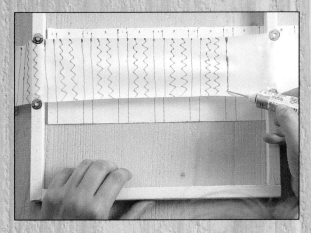 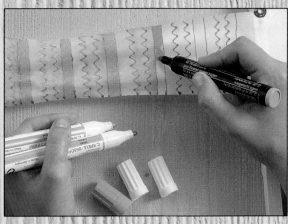 

1 Because of its porous qualities, silk takes paint very well and spreads quickly which can be used to advantage with colour overlapping. Gutta is a resist which stops the spread of paint on silk. Gutta can be obtained in a transparent wax form, as well as in colours and silver or gold. These can be bought in tubes or bottles. Pens, cotton buds and brushes can all be used for painting.

2 The silk should be placed in a frame, either an embroidery or picture frame or a box lid, and pulled taut. Hold the silk with masking tape or silk drawing pins. The silk must not rest on the worktop or the gutta will stick. Work with an even pressure and when finished leave to dry. For speed you can dry gutta with a hairdryer.

3 Paint the design with refillable pens, letting the colours run to produce a further colour. Or use a paintbrush to fill in between the lines of gold gutta, direct from the paint jar.

Spray booth

The best way to contain spray paint and spray glues is to use a cardboard box surrounded by newspaper as a spray booth. An old telephone directory, placed in the box provides a clean base to pin objects to, and helps to stop pieces blowing away. After each spray turn to a clean page.

Covering jewellery backs

Backing brooches and earrings gives them added strength and hides their construction. The backing will provide a better base for gluing or stitching findings in place. Medium weight card or stiff interfacing make good backing materials but may need to be painted. Remember to cut the backing slightly smaller that the actual jewellery. Reverse the back if the jewellery is not symmetrical.

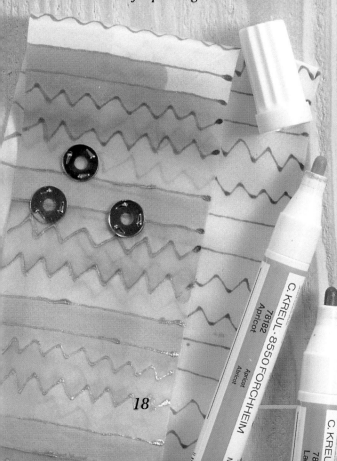

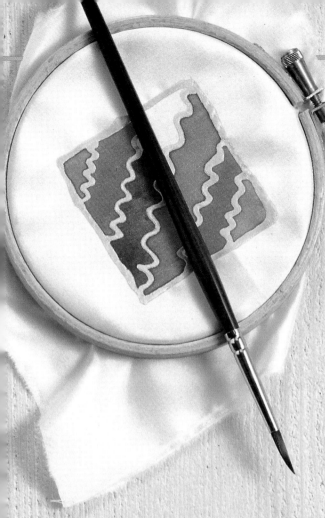

Fusible interfacing

1 *Trace the design onto the fusible interfacing, remembering that it will be reversed when finished. Cut outside the drawn lines, place on the wrong side of motif fabric and bond to fabric by pressing with a steam iron. Leave to cool.*

2 *Cut out the motif following the traced lines. Then peel off the backing paper. Using a steam iron, press the motif onto the main fabric. Leave to cool.*

Wrapping fabric round to the back

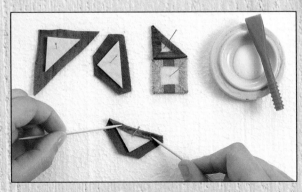

When wrapping fabric round an interfacing or card, cut the fabric 6mm (¹/4in) wider all round. Follow the fabric glue instructions and pin the piece into a polystyrene tile while you ease the seam allowance all round. A couple of orange sticks (or cocktail sticks) will help to hold the fabric in place while the glue dries. Where there is an excess of material, snip, stopping just short of the fold.

Making cords

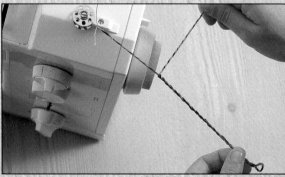

Making cords

Cords can be made with a sewing machine. As a guide 154cm (2¹/4yds) will make a 56cm (22in) cord. Take three yarns, fold in half and slip a polyester thread through fold. Tie thread through bobin slit and place bobin on winder spindle. Holding lengths taut, run the machine so they twist. Find middle, hold, and walk towards machine. The cord will twist, tie, then neaten ends.

19

Cross Stitch

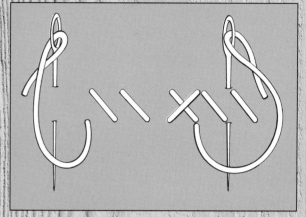

Work each row over two journeys. Work a row of diagonal stitches from right to left, then complete the crosses with a second row of diagonal stitches worked in the opposite direction. Remember that the top diagonal stitches should always slant in the same direction.

Fixing a jumpring

Jumprings are used frequently in the projects in this book. It is important to open jumprings sideways. Use round nosed pliers to do this. Do not pull the jumprings open outwards as they are prone to snap. Now slip the ring through the hole or loop and close the ring.

Fixing a perforated disc

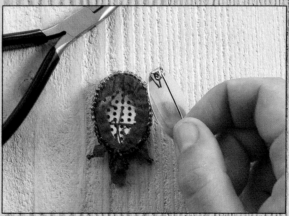

Perforated discs are used with disc shaped brooch backs or clip-on earring backs to make brooches and earrings. The disc can be covered with fabric before you add decoration. Beads can be sewn to the perforated disc or fixed through the holes on headpins. Place the perforated disc over the back and squeeze the claws closed with flat nosed pliers.

Back stitch

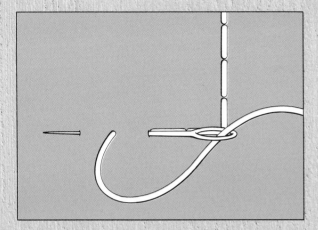

Work back stitch from right to left, making small even stitches forwards and backwards along the row, as shown in the diagram. When using back stitch and cross stitch together, keep the stitches identical in size.

Tent stitch

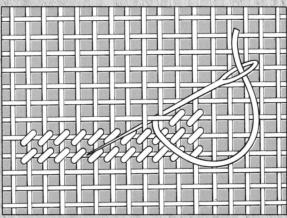

Use the following method for working tent stitch on plastic canvas. Work tent stitch in rows, taking a small stitch on the front of the canvas and a longer one on the reverse.

Overcast stitch

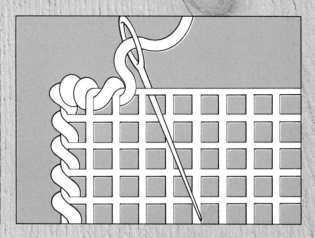

Use overcast stitch to neaten single edges of plastic canvas and to join two pieces. Plastic canvas does not fray, so there is no need to allow turnings — simply align the two edges and stitch together. Work overcast stitch from left to right, taking one stitch through each hole, except at the corners where three stitches are made into the corner hole.

French knot

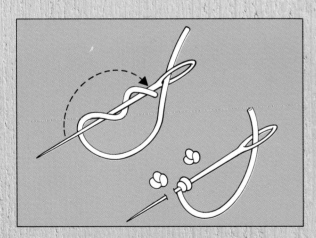

Bring the thread through the fabric and hold it taut with the left hand. Twist the needle round the thread two or three times and tighten the twists. Still holding the thread taut, turn the needle round and insert it in the fabric at the point where it originally emerged. Pull the needle and thread through to the back of the fabric.

Buttonhole stitch

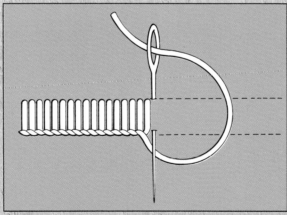

Work buttonhole stitch directly into fabric or over a small brass or plastic ring. Work from left to right, pulling the needle through the fabric over the top of the working thread. Position the stitches close together.

Couching

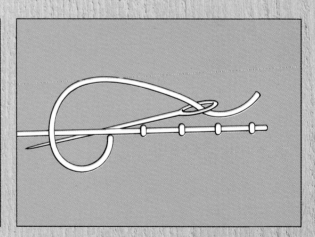

Work from left to right. Lay the thicker thread on the fabric, hold it down with the left hand and anchor it in position with tiny stitches worked in a second finer thread. At the end of the row, pull the thread ends through to the back of the fabric and secure them.

Making a necklace

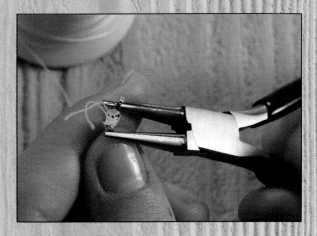
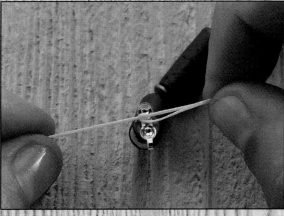

1 *Nylon or cotton thread can be used single or double for extra strength. Use nylon line or tiger tail singly. To start, make a double knot approximately 3.5cm (1¹/2in) from one end. Place the knot in one cup of a calotte crimp. Squeeze the cups together with a pair of flat nosed pliers, enclosing the knot.*

2 *Now thread on the beads. Large beads will hang in a natural curve if the thread is knotted between each bead. Keeping the thread taut, make a double knot close to the last bead. Place the knot in one cup of another calotte crimp and squeeze the cups together as before. Cut off the excess thread close to the cup.*

3 *Open the split loop of the calotte crimps sideways with round nosed pliers and slip onto the loops of the clasp. Close the loops.*

Fixing a boltring fastening

As an alternative necklace fastening to using a clasp or to fasten a bracelet or pendant thong, use a boltring. Follow step 1-2 of Making a Necklace on this page 22. Open the split ring of the calotte crimps sideways with round nosed pliers. Slip a boltring onto one loop and a jumpring or split ring onto the other. Close the loops.

Fixing endclamps

Choose a size of endclamp that fits snugly onto the end of your thong or cord. Slip the endclamp onto the end of the thong. Holding the endclamp securely, squeeze it with flat nosed pliers so that the thong is held tightly. Fasten with a boltring following the Fixing A Boltring Fastening on this page 22.

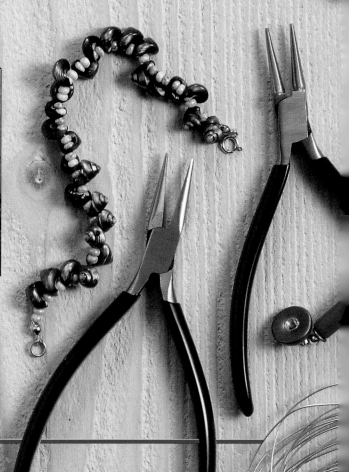

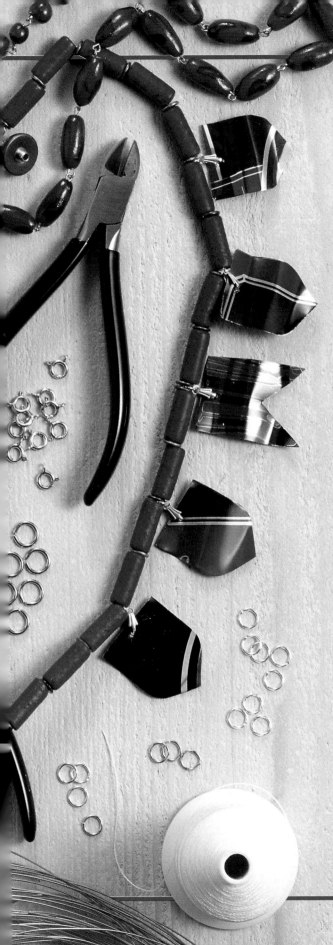

Using a headpin

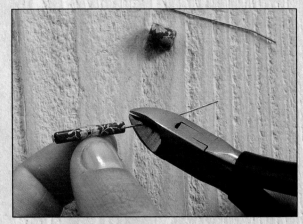

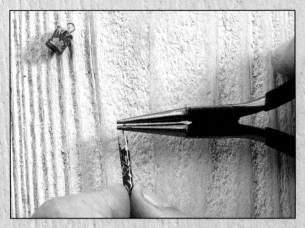

1 *Thread your chosen beads onto a headpin. Start with a small bead if the other bead holes are large. Cut off the excess wire, leaving 6mm (¹/4in) above the last bead.*

2 *With round nosed pliers, bend the wire into a loop, pull the loop towards you as you form it so that it is centred over the last bead.*

Pinning beads

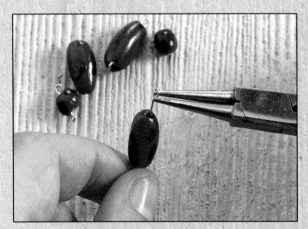

1 *With beads threaded onto wire, use round nosed pliers to bend the wire into a loop at one end. With the bead against the loop, cut off excess wire 6mm (¹/4in) above the bead.*

2 *Make another loop above the bead. To attach pinned beads together, open a loop on one bead, slip on the loop of another bead then reclose the first loop.*

Party Time

Step out in style with this wonderful selection of jewellery for party and evening wear. Jazz up that old black jacket with a glitzy mother of pearl brooch, or add colour with a designer silk brooch. Give a favourite dress a touch of elegance with stunning earrings or make a special occasion even more memorable by creating a piece of jewellery especially for the day.

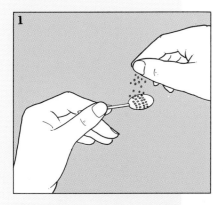

1 Make the gold bead necklace following the Making A Necklace technique on page 22, threading on large gold beads between smaller gold beads. To decorate a bead for the chain necklace push a large glass bead onto a cocktail stick. Apply gold glitter paint in a spiral and sprinkle on gold sequin dust. Insert stick into plastic clay to dry. Shake off the excess sequin dust.

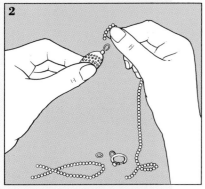

2 Thread the bead onto wire with a small gold bead at each side. Make a loop in the wire at each end following the Pinning Beads technique on page 23. Link each loop to a length of fine chain and fasten with a boltring following the Fixing a Boltring Fastening on page 22.

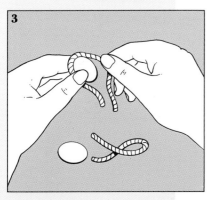

3 To make the oval clip-on earrings, carefully dab a little super glue at the top of a jewellery stone and press on a length of gold cord. Run a line of glue around the oval, knotting the cord below the oval. Dab varnish on the cord ends to prevent fraying, leave to dry then cut the varnished end diagonally. Stick clip-on earring backs to the earring backs with super glue.

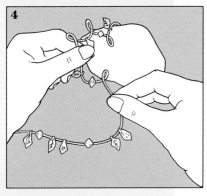

4 To make the mother of pearl brooch, glue the end of a length of gold wire to the back of a piece of mother of pearl shell with craft glue. Thread on glass beads and gold leaf charms. Drape the wire around the shell, bending the wire into loops and gluing occasionally to the shell to hold it in place. Glue the wire end to the shell back. Use craft glue to stick a brooch pin to the back.

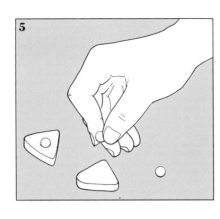

6 *Gloss varnish the triangles. Glue the bead to the centre with super glue. Use a needle to thread 16 strands of fine gold thread through the bead, separate into 2 bunches of 8 strands and fasten together securely on the back of the triangle. Dab threads with super glue to secure in place. Glue clip-on earring backs to the backs of the earrings.*

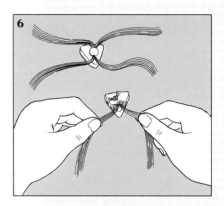

5 *Roll two 2cm (³/4in) diameter balls of air-drying clay for the triangular earrings. Flatten to 6mm (¹/4in) thick and mould into triangles. Make a depression in the centre with a gold bead. Indent the triangle edges with a knife to make a row of cuts. Set aside to harden, then paint with white pearlized craft paint.*

◀ *Shades of gold and turquoise set off this range of stylish jewellery to great effect. Various materials have been used to make the pieces, from ready made beads, to air-drying clay and even plastic curtain rings.*

7 *To make the paisley shaped earrings, roll air-drying clay out flat 6mm (¹/4in) thick. Cut a pair of paisley shapes. Lay a long bead on top and pierce a hole at each end and at the top. Decorate the surface with a pin. Indent the edges with a knife to make a row of cuts. Leave to harden then paint with gold craft paint. Gloss varnish the shapes.*

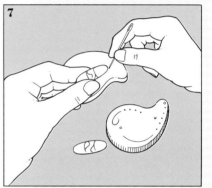

8 *Sew the beads to the earrings with gold thread, knotting the threads together on the back. Fix a large jumpring to the top hole. Thread a round bead onto wire with a small gold bead at each side. Make a loop in the wire at each end following the Pinning to Beads technique on page 23. Fix the loop to the jumprings and earring wires.*

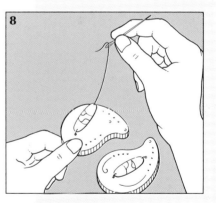

9 *To make the ring earrings, unscrew the screw eye in two plastic curtain rings. Drill a hole through the ring, thread with gold wire. Bind the wire around the ring, threading on glass and gold beads and gold leaf shaped charms. Occasionally bend the wire into small loops. Twist the wire ends together on top of the ring. Cut off one end, thread on a diamanté spacer and two gold beads. Make a loop on top and fix to earring wires.*

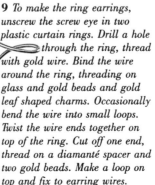

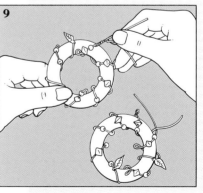

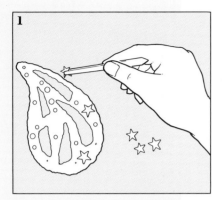

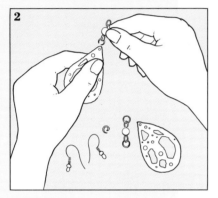

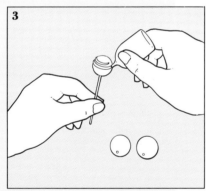

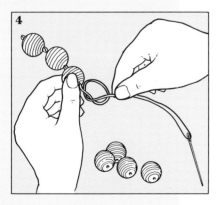

1 To make the pendant and silver drop earrings, use an old pair of scissors to cut thin sheets of metal into teardrop and paisley shapes. Pierce a hole at the top. Apply glitter paint, leaving gaps so that the metal shows through. Position tiny sequin stars and small jewellery stones into the glitter with tweezers.

2 Press the decorations into the glitter and leave to dry. Apply glitter paint to two small beads for the earrings. Thread the pendant with a thong and follow the Fixing Endclamps technique on page 22 to finish the pendant. Thread wire through the glittery beads and make a loop at each end following the Pinning Beads technique on page 23. Fix a jumpring to one loop, attach to the earring. Fix a jumpring to the other loop. Fix to earring wire.

3 To make a long necklace pierce a hole through twenty-seven 2cm (³/4in) and ten 1.5cm (⁵/8in) diameter cotton pulp balls, which are available from craft stores. Push the balls onto cocktail sticks to decorate. Apply glitter paint in random stripes on the balls using different colours. Insert sticks into plastic clay to dry.

4 With the small beads at each end, thread the beads onto a long double length of glittering yarn, knotting the yarn between each bead. Fasten the necklace following the Fixing A Boltring Fastening technique on page 22.

▶ Glitter paints, shiny metals and glossy paints add sparkle and glitz to these glistening jewellery pieces.

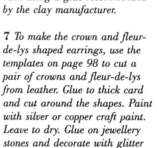

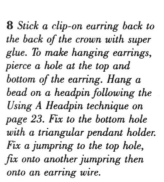

5 *Scrunch up aluminium foil to cover a plastic bangle, squeezing it to fit. Any loose ends can be stuck in place with all-purpose household glue. Paint the bangle in diagonal stripes using transparent glass paints. Set aside to dry.*

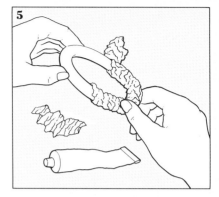

6 *Mould coloured plastic clay that will harden in the oven into a paisley shape to make the blue glittering brooch. Wrap a small make-up mirror in an old towel and smash with a hammer to break it into fragments. Arrange the fragments and glass jewellery stones on top, then press the pieces into the clay to embed them. Bake in the oven following the clay manufacturer's instructions. Decorate with glitter paints. Stick a brooch back to the back using a glue recommended by the clay manufacturer.*

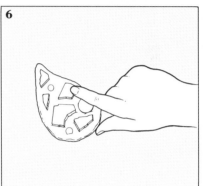

7 *To make the crown and fleur-de-lys shaped earrings, use the templates on page 98 to cut a pair of crowns and fleur-de-lys from leather. Glue to thick card and cut around the shapes. Paint with silver or copper craft paint. Leave to dry. Glue on jewellery stones and decorate with glitter paints.*

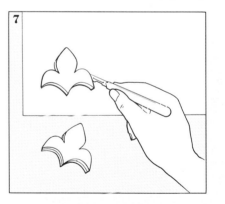

8 *Stick a clip-on earring back to the back of the crown with super glue. To make hanging earrings, pierce a hole at the top and bottom of the earring. Hang a bead on a headpin following the Using A Headpin technique on page 23. Fix to the bottom hole with a triangular pendant holder. Fix a jumpring to the top hole, fix onto another jumpring then onto an earring wire.*

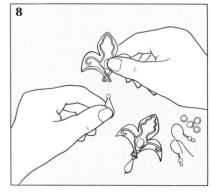

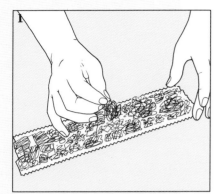

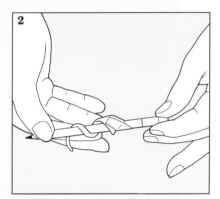

1 *To make the bracelet, cut a length of stiff interfacing to fit your wrist then trim around edge with pinking sheers. Paint or sponge the front, back and edges and leave to dry. Scatter scraps of brightly coloured fabric and threads onto the interfacing, and following the Free Machine Embroidery technique on page 16, randomly sew the scraps to the interfacing using contrasting threads until all the pieces are firmly held. Neaten thread ends. Line bracelet back with a strip of ribbon. Use touch and close tape to make the bracelet fastening.*

2 *To make the spiral earrings, draw around the template on page 98. Transfer the design onto soluble fabric and following the Sewing On Cold Water Soluble Fabric technique on pages 16-17, machine embroider the area. Coil the embroidered lengths by wrapping them around a pencil and leave to dry. When the lengths are dry, attach a small bead and fix to an earring wire.*

3 *For the heart earrings, trace the templates on page 98 and cut out in stiff interfacing. Cover the interfacing with foil sweet papers using a dab of glue to position. Wrap a layer of chiffon over the papers. Following the Free Machine Embroidery technique on page 16, sew with straight stitch over each heart until the papers are attached. Neaten thread ends. Edge the heart following the Couching technique on page 21, couching with a different coloured thread. Line backs with a shaped, silver painted piece of stiff interfacing. Attach a bead and earring wire to each earring. Make the brooch in the same way, but use the larger template, and attach a brooch pin to the back.*

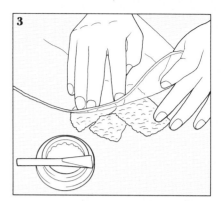

4 *To make the bronze cross earrings, trace the template on pages 98-99 and cut out in stiff interfacing. Sponge the interfacing with bronze fabric paint and leave to dry. Following the Free Machine Embroidery technique on page 16, sew from the centre out, using embroidery thread. Decorate with beads and attach stud fastenings to the cross backs. Make the brooch in the same way. Stiffen it with a backing of interfacing and add a brooch pin.*

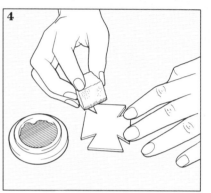

5 *To make the choker, trace the template on page 98 and cut out in stiff interfacing. Sponge with fabric paint and leave to dry. Following the Free Machine Embroidery technique on page 16 and using shaded machine embroidery threads, sew around the collar with swirly designs.*

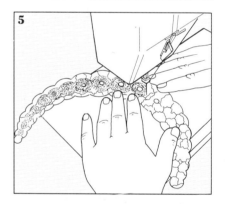

6 *Using four thin cords, make a tie for the collar following the Making Cords technique on page 19. Leave areas of cords showing and bind twice more. Machine stitch the ties to the collar. Cover ends by coiling thin cord in a circle held with fabric glue. Finish by brushing the edges and centre holes of the collar with bronze fabric paint.*

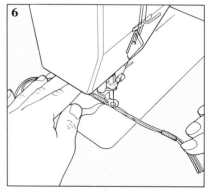

31

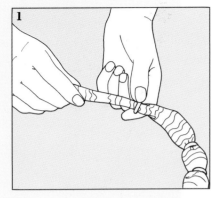

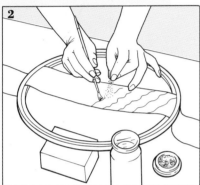

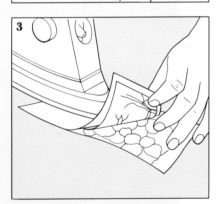

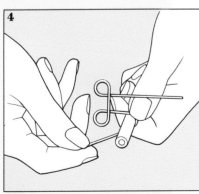

1 *To make the necklace, draw up a grid with rules spaced 1 x 3cm (³/8 x ¹/8in) apart. Cut a 59 x 7.5cm (23 x 2³/4in) bias strip of Haboutai silk following Step 1 of Making a Rouleau technique on page 17. Place silk in a frame over the grid lines and using gutta draw in the lines without touching the grid. Leave to dry. Paint between the gutta with silk pens. Once dry press on the wrong side with a steam iron. Following the Making A Rouleau technique on page 17, make into a bias tube. Push a cotton ball through the tube to the centre, so that it fills the centre zig-zag pattern. Thread a spacer bead on either side of this, then thread eight more balls and spacers through the tube, ending with spacers. Turn in the tube ends, slipstitch and tie necklace to fit.*

2 *To make the bangles cut a 28 x 7.5cm (11 x 3in) bias strip of Haboutai silk. Place the silk in an embroidery frame. Using three coloured silk paints and some rock salt, paint diagonal lines and sprinkle with the salt while the paint is wet. The salt will leave patterns in the silk. Once dry, shake off the salt and press the fabric using a steam iron to set the colour. Following the Making A Rouleau technique on page 17, make the tube, then fill the tube with 6 cotton balls and 7 spacers. Depending on the size of your wrist you may need another ball. Turn in the ends, then tie the bracelet in a decorative knot.*

3 *To make the silk brooches, place a wet piece of Haboutai silk into a frame. Apply small dots of silk paint to the fabric allowing the paint to run. Once dry, press the silk on the wrong side using a steam iron which will fix the paint. To add the silver designs, cover the ironing board with a sheet of paper, place the silk fabric on the paper right side up, position the foil dots on the silk and cover with a second sheet of*

paper. Iron for 10-30 seconds on the silk/wool setting, or until the dots have transferred to the fabric. Select the brooch area, and, following manufacturer's instructions, mount the silk in the brooch frame.*

4 *To make the bonsai wire and silk earrings, cut a length of middle-weight bonsai florist wire 15cm (6in) long. Form four circles around a pencil following the shape shown in the diagram. Trim ends so that they butt up.*

5 *Cut a 10cm (4in) square strip of Haboutai silk on the bias following Step 1 of Making A Rouleau technique on page 17. Place in an embroidery frame and draw fine lines with gutta 6mm (¹/4in) apart. When dry, use a paintbrush to fill in between the lines. Once dry, fix with a steam iron. Cut the fabric into strips to fit across the wire. Glue one end of the strip in place, using the end of a pin as the glue applicator. Then wrap the strip across the wire and finish with another line of glue. Attach to an earring wire.*

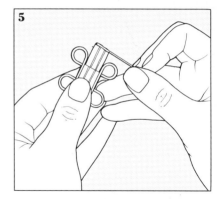

6 *To make the fish choker, draw around the template on page 99 using a fine pencil and transfer to a piece of Haboutai silk which is large enough to fit a small embroidery frame. Cut a second piece of silk 46 x 10cm (18 x 4in) for the sea. Place both pieces of silk into embroidery frames and pull taut, holding with masking tape. Draw around the fish outline and draw in waves on the second piece of silk using silver gutta. Leave to dry. Paint with silk paint and leave to dry. Once dry, fix with a steam iron. Sew the long sides of the sea strip together and turn through. Cut a piece of stiff interfacing to fit around your neck and the same width as the strip. Insert the interfacing into the sea strip, slipstitch ends closed and attach touch and close tape as a fastening.*

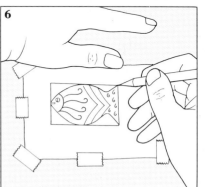

7 *Iron the fusible paper on to the wrong side of the fish, cut around just outside the silver gutta line, then attach to stiff interfacing with an iron. Machine stitch with silver thread around the outliner using straight stitch. Cover the stitches with a narrow satin stitch. Carefully trim just outside the stitching line. Attach the fish to the sea choker with lengths of silver beads, ensuring they are firmly sewn at the ends.*

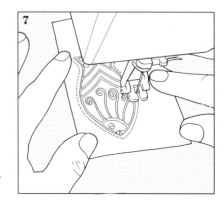

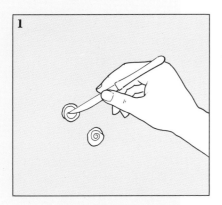

1 Prepare the papier mâché pulp (which is available from art and craft stores) following the manufacturer's instructions. To make the spiral clip-on earrings, roll a 2cm (^{3}/4in) diameter ball of pulp for each earring. Flatten the balls and indent a spiral with a knife tip.

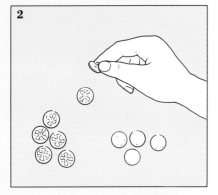

2 To make the discs for the bracelet and tasselled earrings, roll 1.5cm (^{5}/8in) balls of pulp. Flatten and press a textured button onto the centre to emboss the discs. Pierce a hole at the lower edge for the two earring discs. Pierce two holes at opposite sides of the bracelet discs.

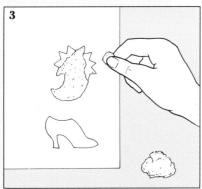

3 To make the tassels, blue cartouche shaped earrings, shoe stick pin and cornucopia brooch, draw around the templates on page 99 with a ballpoint pen onto a sheet of plastic. Build up the pulp within the outlines to 6mm (^{1}/4in) thick. Indent the details on the tassels with a knife tip and pierce a hole at the top.

4 Emboss the cartouches with a textured button, dab the top of a heart shaped bead with PVA medium and insert into the bottom of the cartouches. Dab gold beads with PVA medium and press into the outer points. Pierce a horizontal hole at the dot on the shoes for the stick pin. Stick a gold button and a row of bugle beads to the shoe with PVA medium. Dab coloured beads with PVA medium and press into the shoe at random.

5 *Stick a row of bugle beads across the cornucopia with PVA medium. Dab gold beads with PVA medium and press into the pulp. Roll a small ball of pulp and stick to the point with PVA medium. Cut two large and two small cornucopia flowers from card using the template on page 99. Also cut a few small leaf shapes from card. Arrange the flowers, leaves, some beads and a gold leaf shaped charm on the brooch. Stick in position with PVA medium.*

6 *Set all the models aside to harden, then paint with Indian inks. Fine details can be painted with gold Indian ink. To highlight the jewellery, rub on some gold wax (available from art stores). Varnish the models with clear matt varnish. Stick clip-on earring backs to the back of the spiral and cartouche earrings with super glue. Fix jumprings to the tassels.*

7 *Link discs for the bracelet together with large jumprings, fix a large jumpring to each end and fasten with a boltring following the Fixing A Boltring Fastening technique on page 22. To make the tasselled necklace, thread blue glass beads onto thread, positioning the three pulp tassels in the centre, making up the necklace following the Making A Necklace technique on page 22.*

8 *To finish the tasselled earrings, fix the jumprings on the tassels through the holes in the discs, then super glue a flat pad earstud to the back. Dab super glue on the top of a stick pin and insert into the hole in the shoe. Super glue a brooch pin to the back of the cornucopia.*

◄ *This richly coloured papier mâché jewellery has a regal air. The papier mâché can be embellished with beads as simply or as lavishly as you wish.*

5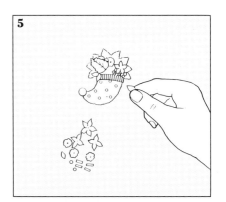

6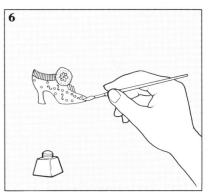

7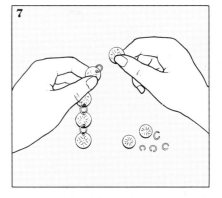

8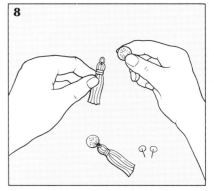

Going Natural

For the county lover, a range of jewellery which really goes back to nature. Twigs, paper and shells are all used to make superb and decorative items to enhance any outfit. A country walk can become an earring hunt, and gathering driftwood from beaches for necklaces and brooches will soon become second nature.

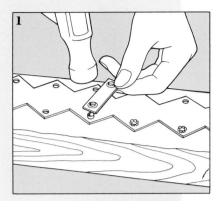

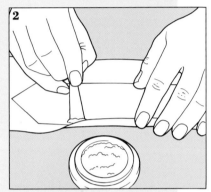

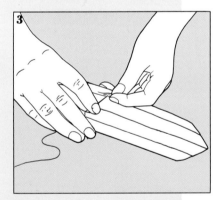

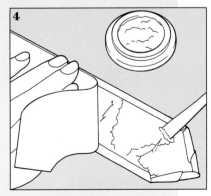

1 *To make the suede choker, draw around the template on page 100. Using small pieces of double-sided tape position the template on the wrong side of the split suede. Using a sharp craft knife cut out two chokers. Also cut out four thongs 16cm (6¹/2in) long. Mark the eyelet positions on the chokers, then punch holes and insert the eyelets. Glue the two chokers together covering the backs of the eyelets and trim any untidy edges. Make four holes for the thongs, thread the thongs through and knot to hold them in place.*

2 *To make the leather bangle, cut a piece of stiff interfacing 5 x 24cm (2 x 9¹/2in), cutting the interfacing into a point at one end. Cut a piece of gloving leather 13 x 26cm (5¹/4 x 10¹/4in). Lay the leather right side down, and place the stiff interfacing on top. Taking in a narrow hem, glue along the wrong sides of both long edges to attach the leather to the interfacing. Leave to dry.*

3 *Turn the bangle over and carefully manipulate the extra leather into four horizontal pleats. Catch stitch under the pleats every 5cm (2in), taking care to ensure the stitches do not show. At each end, trim and fold the leather to the back and glue in place.*

4 *Glue a strip of contrasting gloving leather to the back of the bangle and add touch and close tape at each end.*

5 *To make the brooch and earrings, cut out gloving leather 1.5cm (³/4in) larger than the earring or base. Using a double thickness of polyester thread, start in the centre, knot the thread and thread one bead, passing your needle through the centre of the pierced disc. Next sew around the edge of the pierced disc, ruching stitches and sewing on a bead each time you take a stitch. Continue ruching, manipulating the leather until it is evenly covered with beads. Attach the backing for the brooch and earrings by levering the prongs over the pierced disc.*

6 *To make the rolled pendant, trace the templates on pages 99-100 on the reverse side of leather and cut out. Glue the wrong side of the turquoise leather to the right side of the gold leather, leaving a 3mm (¹/8in) edge. Place a few dabs of glue along the centre of the pendant to hold the leather in place. Then start rolling from the wide gold end, use a knitting needle. Check that the edges are parallel. When completely rolled, hold for a minute until the glue has set. Also roll up the small bead.*

7 *Loop a 1m (39in) thong around the pendant, then thread on beads to hold it in place.*

8 *Before making a watchstrap, check the bar measurements of the watch. This watch has a bar 2cm (³/4in) wide. Cut a strip of fine gloving leather 7 x 28cm (2³/4 x 11in), shaping the ends so that they will pass through the buckle. Thread the strap through the watch bars, then gather one end into a buckle without a prong, and sew the buckle to the leather using a leather needle. Spread out the leather and draw a series of triangles, stars, bars and spirals to make an all-over pattern using gold marker pen.*

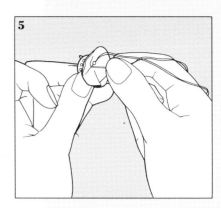
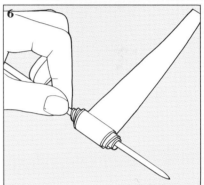
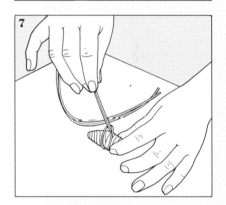
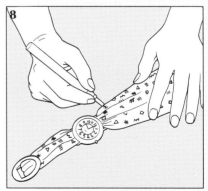

1 *To make the pinwheel hatpin, cut out strips of felt in three different colours all 1.5 x 21.5cm (³/4 x 8¹/2in). Glue one strip on top of the other, layering them so that they roll neatly from one end.*

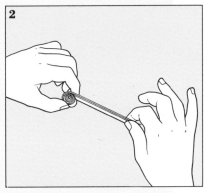

2 *Once the glue has dried, roll the wad tightly from the bottom layer and gluing the strip to itself as you roll. Leave felt roll to dry. To finish, thread two beads onto a collar or hat pin, then carefully push the pin through the pinwheel.*

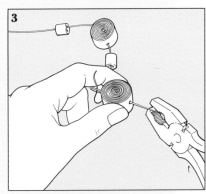

3 *Following the instructions to make a pinwheel hatpin, make five pinwheels. Using a crewel needle and a silky thread, string the pinwheels onto the thread, spacing the pinwheels with wooden barrel beads. As the pinwheels are tightly glued, a pair of pliers may help to pull the needle through. Finish off with wooden beads on both sides, then attach a clasp to the thread following the Making A Necklace technique on page 22.*

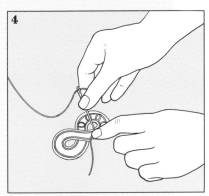

4 *To make the figure of eight brooch, trace the template on page 100 onto orange and red felt and stiff interfacing. Cut out one piece of felt slightly larger than the other. Trace the inner shapes onto the smaller piece. Glue the larger piece onto the interfacing, then add the smaller piece and leave to dry. Couch yellow bourdon cord in a figure of eight shape, adding twisted circles and filling in with beads. Use a felt tip to colour in backing edges. Glue on a brooch fitting.*

5 *To make the daisy earrings, draw around the template on page 100 and cut out two orange and two purple daisy shapes and centres. Also cut out the daisy shapes in card or stiff interfacing. Glue an orange daisy to one side of the card and a purple daisy to the other. Glue the centres in contrasting colours. When the glue is dry, trim any excess felt and backing and colour the backing edge with a felt tip pen. Using polyester thread, sew a daisy petal and thread three wooden beads. Pass the thread through an earring wire and back through the beads. Stitch to secure.*

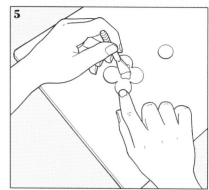

6 *To make the felt bracelet, cut strips 2 x 7cm (1³/4 x 2³/4in) from felt in a range of colours from red through orange to yellow. Thread a length of hat elastic onto a chenille needle. Fold the strips into a zig-zag shape and sew through the centre of each. Work, grading the colours, until you have made a length to fit your wrist. Tie the elastic ends in a knot, trim, then twist the felt pieces in a random pattern so you have a mixture of ends and folds.*

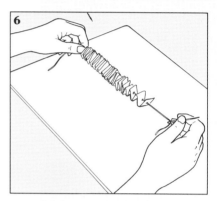

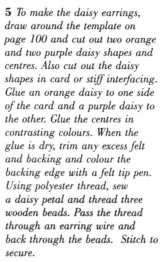

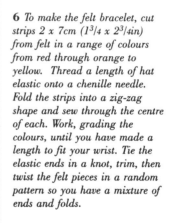

◀ *Felt is a fabulous fabric to work with as it never frays. Here it makes bright accessories for everyday wear.*

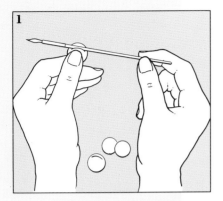

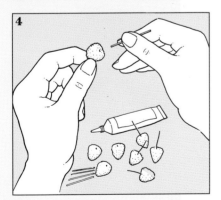

1 *To make the cherry earrings, roll four 2cm (³/4in) diameter balls of red, oven-hardening clay. Make a depression in the top and underside by pressing a paintbrush across the clay. Pierce a hole in the top with a needle. Bake cherries following the manufacturer's instructions. Cut two 10cm (4in) lengths of thick wire and bend in half forming a loop at the top. Glue ends into the cherries. Paint the wire green. Gloss varnish the earrings. Fix a large jumpring to the wire loop and fix to an earring wire.*

2 *To make the lemon and lime brooch and strawberries, prepare papier mâché pulp (which is available from art and craft stores) following manufacturer's instructions. Draw the brooch template on page 100 with a ballpoint pen onto a sheet of plastic. Build up the pulp within the vase outline. Mould the fruits from pulp and arrange within the drawn outline.*

3 *Leave to harden, then smooth more pulp onto the underside to even out the surface. Set aside to harden. Paint with Indian inks. Rub on some gold wax (available from art stores) to highlight the brooch. Apply three coats of matt varnish. Super glue a brooch pin to the back.*

4 *Mould papier mâché pulp into eight ovals 2cm (³/4in) long for the strawberries. Squeeze one end to narrow them. Pierce the top with a thick needle. Leave to harden, dab the end of 3.5cm (1¹/2in) lengths of gold wire with super glue and insert into the holes. Paint the strawberries with red poster paint.*

▶ *Ripe for picking, this fruit and vegetable inspired jewellery looks good enough to eat. Make stunning clay cherry earrings, necklaces hung with blackberries or strawberries or stylish black aubergine earrings.*

5 *To make blackberries, squeeze cling film (plastic wrap) into fourteen oval balls 2cm (³/4in) long. Dab the end of 3.5cm (1¹/2in) lengths of gold wire with craft glue, push into the top of the ovals. Dab ovals with craft glue and use tweezers to stick on polystyrene ballbearings (available for filling toys and cushions at sewing suppliers). Squeeze the ballbearings tightly together. Paint with craft paints; green and red paint can be used to suggest unripened fruits.*

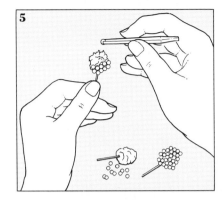

6 *Use the templates on page 101 to cut a sepal for each fruit from green fabric. Pierce a hole through the centre of the sepals and thread onto the fruit wires. Stick to the top of the fruits with craft glue. Matt varnish the pieces. Bend wires into loops on top of the sepals and cut off excess. Make up the necklace following the Making a Necklace Technique on page 22. Thread the strawberries amongst yellow beads and flower shaped beads. Thread blackberries amongst gold beads and leaf shaped charms.*

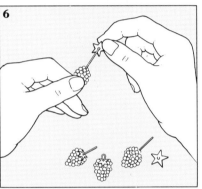

7 *To decorate a plastic bangle, first paint the bangle with blue pearlized craft paint. Use craft paints to paint fronds of leaves and raspberries. Apply a thin film of gold craft paint to an old plate. Dab at the paint with a dampened natural sponge. Dab the sponge onto the bangle to lightly apply the paint. Coat with satin varnish.*

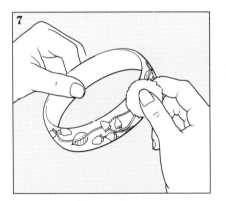

8. *To make the aubergine earrings, super glue an ornate pendant holder with a hole to the top of a black drop bead. Fix to earring wires.*

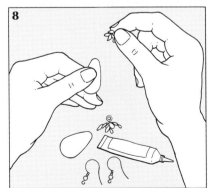

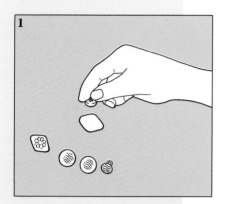

1 To make the earrings, roll air-drying clay into a ball, then roll out flat to make discs or mould the clay into diamond shapes. Press a textured button onto the clay to emboss a design. To hang the pieces, either pierce a hole at the top or punch a hole with a drinking straw. Indent the circumference of the earrings and punched holes with a pinhead.

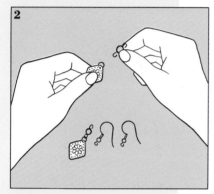

2 Roll a 8mm (⁵/₁₆in) ball of clay for each earring; these can also be embossed with a button. Pierce a hole through the centre. Set aside to harden. Fix a large jumpring through the holes on the earrings. Thread each bead onto wire. A ceramic bead was added for the natural coloured clay earrings. Make a loop in the wire at each end of the beads following the Pinning Beads technique on page 23. Fix the pinned beads to the jumprings and earring wires or earstuds.

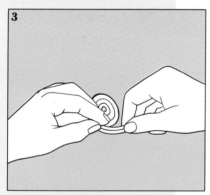

3 To make the ring, roll thin sausages of natural and terracotta air-drying clay. Press the sausages together and arrange in a spiral. Squeeze into an oval. Set aside to harden, then stick to a ring with super glue.

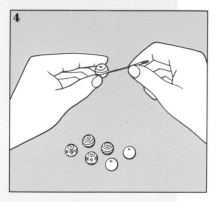

4 To make the beige necklace, roll twenty 1.5cm (⁵/₈in) diameter balls of terracotta clay. Pierce a hole through the centre. Leave to harden. Paint the beads with unbleached titanium acrylic paint. When the paint has dried, use a thick needle to scratch a pattern on the beads. Matt varnish the beads. A coat of varnish will also protect the other clay pieces. Make up the necklace following the Making A Necklace technique on page 22, threading on a few glass or plastic beads between the clay beads.

5 *Roll terracotta air-drying clay out flat 6mm (¹/4in) thick with a rolling pin for the animal pendant. Cut a simple animal shape using a knife, then indent the animal all over with the head of a pin. Roll a 6mm (¹/4in) thick sausage of clay and cut two 6mm (¹/4in) slices. Pierce a hole on the animal's back and through the beads. Leave to harden.*

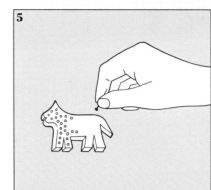

6 *Fix a pendant holder through the hole on the animal. Fix a jumpring to the pendant holder. Follow the Making A Necklace technique on page 22 to make up the necklace with small gold beads, adding the terracotta beads 2cm (³/4in) from the centre. Use two cream beads at the centre placing the animal between them.*

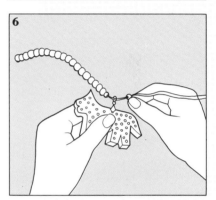

7 *Roll eight 2.5cm (1in) diameter balls of terracotta air-drying clay. Roll tiny balls of natural clay, flatten then moisten and press to the balls to make the spotted necklace. Roll the balls again to embed the spots. Roll thirteen 1cm (³/8in) diameter balls of natural clay. Flatten three of the natural balls to form circular discs.*

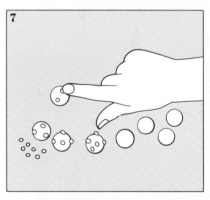

8 *Pierce a hole through all the beads, then set aside to harden. Follow the Making A Necklace technique on page 22, positioning the spotted beads and discs in the centre. Add the round natural beads then small cream beads. A small bead between the large clay beads will help the necklace lay in a smooth curve.*

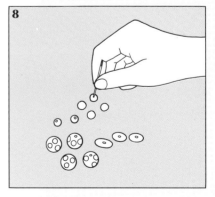

◄ *Natural terracotta and stone coloured clay give an earthy feel to these ethnic jewellery pieces.*

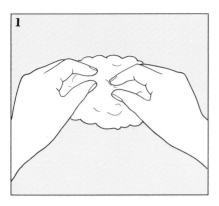

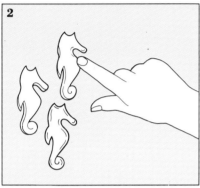

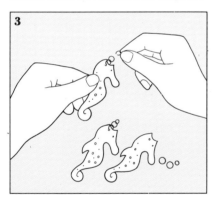

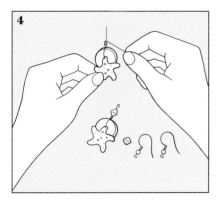

1 *The seahorses and starfishes are made from salt dough. To make the dough, mix together 10 tablespoons of plain flour, 5 tablespoons of salt and 3 tablespoons of water. Gradually add another 2 tablespoons of water as you knead the mixture to a firm dough. When all the ingredients are thoroughly mixed, knead for a further 5 minutes.*

2 *The starfishes have been coloured with food colouring. Break off a third of the dough, add a few drops of blue food colouring and knead until completely blended. Roll the dough out flat 6mm (1/4in) thick. Use the templates on page 101 to cut three seahorses and a pair of starfishes. Pat the cut edges to curve them. Pierce a hole at the top. Indent the eyes, then indent at random with a pin. Bake in the oven at 120°C/ 250°F/Gas Mark 1/2 for six hours.*

3 *Fix the seahorses to two large jumprings, then fix to a small jumpring. Follow the Making A Necklace technique on page 22 to make the seahorse necklace, threading on small aquamarine, mother of pearl and ceramic beads. Position the seahorses in the centre 4cm (11/2in) apart.*

4 *To make the starfish earrings, cut a bottle cork into two 6mm (1/4in) slices. Pierce a hole through the centre and thread with wire. Thread on a starfish. Lift up the wire ends and twist together above the cork. Cut off one end of the wire. Thread on a bead and make a loop on top of the bead. Fix onto an earring wire.*

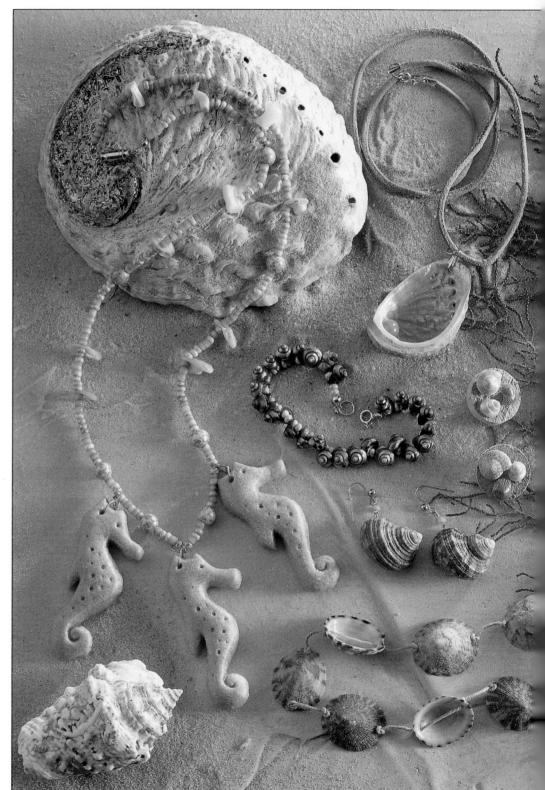

◀ *Take inspiration from the seashore to make this range of handsome jewellery. Make up the pieces with beachcombed shells to remind you of favourite holidays.*

5 *To make the shell drop earrings, drill a hole in two shells – embed the shells in plastic clay to steady them whilst drilling. Fix three small beads onto wire following the Pinning Beads technique on page 23. Fix the loops to the shells and earring wires.*

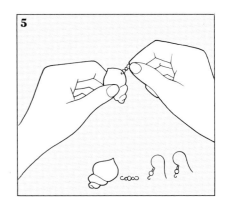

6 *To make the shell bracelet, drill holes in approximately thirty small shells. Make up the bracelet following the Fixing A Boltring technique on page 22, placing two small beads between each shell. To make the clip-on cork earrings, cut a bottle cork into two 6mm (¹/4in) slices. Stick small shells on top, then stick a clip-on earring back to the underside with super glue.*

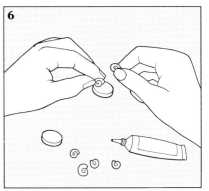

7 *To make the shell necklace, drill a hole in each side of twenty-three shells. Thread onto linen yarn, knotting the yarn against each shell. Knot the yarn ends together on the underside of the shells.*

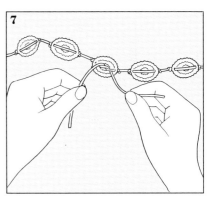

8 *To make the pendant, stick a coloured pearl bead in a shell with super glue. Fix a pendant holder through a hole at the top of the shell. Fix a large jumpring to the pendant holder. Thread onto suede thonging. Follow the Fixing Endclamps technique on page 22 to finish the pendant.*

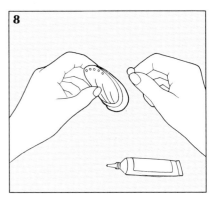

47

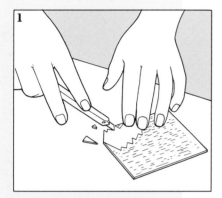

1 *To make the serrated earings trace the template on page 101 and cut out in thin 2mm (¹/8in) thick balsa wood using a craft knife. Paint the wood with two or three coats of silk or fabric paint, leaving the paint to dry between coats. Seal the paint with a couple of coats of clear nail polish or varnish. Glue on three flat wooden beads, then finish by attaching earring studs to the narrow end.*

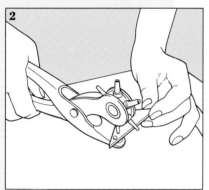

2 *To make the arrow brooch, trace the template on page 101 and cut out in thin balsa wood. Also cut a thin backing card and glue the two together using a clear glue. Mark where the holes should be, then punch them.*

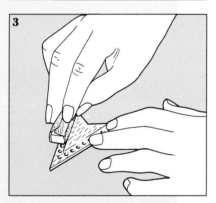

3 *Wrap fine grade sandpaper around a block and rub down along the lines of each of the holes, forming an arrow shape in the centre. Use matt varnish to paint the brooch and attach a brooch pin on the back.*

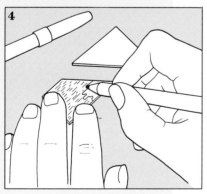

4 *To make the three dimensional brooch, trace the templates on page 101 and cut out the seven pieces in thin balsa wood. The circular shape is the wooden bead. Colour the wood using felt tip pens or gouache and once dry assemble the brooch using clear glue and following the finished piece as a guide. Attach a brooch fitting to the back.*

5 *To make the twig and feather brooch, cut a 6cm (2^{1}/2in) square of balsa wood. Rub the square down with fine sandpaper and slightly round the corners. Colour the square with silk paint, gouache or felt tip pen. Cut seven twigs 5cm (2in) long and shave one side off each one so that they will lie flat. Assemble the twigs, then attach them with a thin coat of clear glue. Leave to dry, then attach a feather and add a brooch mount to the back.*

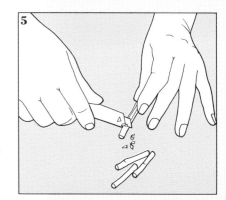

6 *To make the drop earrings, cut two pieces of balsa wood 5.5 x 2cm (2^{1}/4 x ^{3}/4in). Trim seven coloured matchsticks to 3.5cm (1^{1}/2in). Attach to the earring backs using thin coats of clear glue. When dry varnish. Use gold wire to make a link, add a jumpring and attach gold earring wires.*

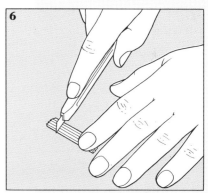

7 *To make the driftwood pendant you will need a small piece of driftwood. Using gouache, paint the driftwood in a random way to suggest the colour has worn off through exposure. Once dry, cover the wood with a couple of coats of matt varnish. Drill a small hole for the pendant finding. Adapt an earring wire to make the fixing, then thread with a matching thong.*

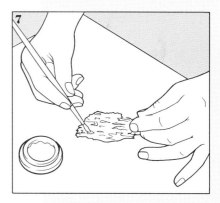

◀ *Balsa wood can be used to make all sorts of different shapes, so once you get used to cutting the wood why not try making curved or circular items.*

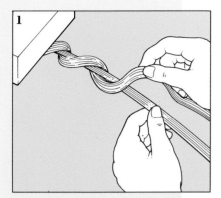

1 *To make the necklace cut seven 75cm (29in) lengths of raffia in four colours. Bunch together at one end and bind tightly with thread. Dab with glue to secure. Place a heavy weight on the fastened end. Separate three strands of raffia and stretch out straight. Wrap the other strands around the stretched strands. Bind the thread tightly around the raffia ends, dab with glue and cut off the surplus raffia. Thread on a large plastic bead.*

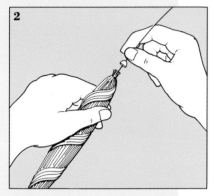

2 *Fasten a length of polycotton thread securely to one end and thread a jewellery cap on top. Tie a torpedo clasp on top of the cap and thread needle back through the cap. Cut off the thread. Finish the other end of the necklace in the same way.*

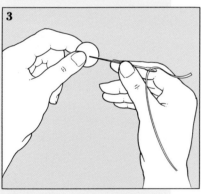

3 *To make the tasselled earrings, cut two circles of thick card 2.5cm (1in) in diameter. Pierce a hole through the centre. Thread red raffia on a needle, insert through the hole and glue the end to the back of the circle. Apply glue to the right side, coil the raffia around the hole and stick in place. Glue the end of the raffia to the back.*

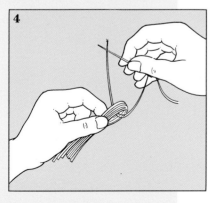

4 *To make the tassels, cut 12 pieces of raffia 19cm (7¹/2in) in length for each earring. Thread a needle with polycotton thread and knot the ends together. Bunch the raffia together and fold in half. Slip the needle under the fold and insert between the threads. Pull tightly, enclosing the raffia. Insert the needle up through a jewellery cap and glue the threads to the back of the circle. Trim the raffia ends level. Glue a clip-on earring back to the back of the circle.*

◀ *Brighten your holiday wardrobe with raffia jewellery in warm and sunny tones of colour.*

5 Bind narrow plastic bangles with two lengths of contrasting-coloured raffia, gluing the ends to the bangle to start and finish. Bind a wide coloured plastic bangle with raffia and glue the ends in place. Thread raffia on a needle and weave three rows in and out of the binding. Glue the ends to the bangle.

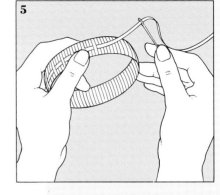

6 To make the bracelet, cut four pieces of raffia 26cm (10¼in) in length in three colours. Bunch together at one end and bind tightly with thread. Dab with glue to secure the ends together. Use a hand drill to make a hole in six small shells. Thread the shells onto six strands of the raffia. Bind thread tightly around the raffia ends, dab with glue and cut off the excess raffia. Finish the bracelet in the same way as Step 2.

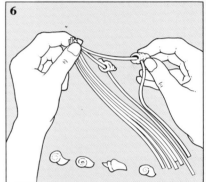

7 Cover a hairclip by binding it closely with raffia, gluing the ends on the underside. Then bind with a contrasting coloured raffia back and forth to make a criss-cross pattern. Glue shells to the top as a decoration.

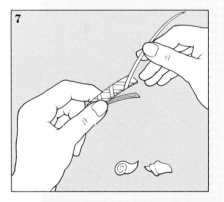

8 Cut four circles of thin card 4.5cm (1¾in) in diameter for the hanging disc earrings. Pierce a hole through the centre of two circles. Draw a circle 1.5cm (⅝in) in diameter, then another 2.5cm (1in) in diameter on the pierced circles. Thread orange raffia on a needle, insert through the hole and glue the end to the back of the circle. Apply glue to the inner circle, coil the raffia around the hole and stick in place. Cut off surplus raffia. Apply glue to the remainder of the circle. Stick yellow raffia to the middle ring, then beige raffia to the outer circle. Glue the other circles to the back of the discs and pierce a hole through the top. Fix to earring wires with pendant holders and jumprings.

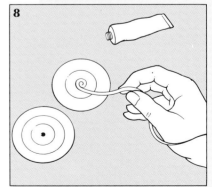

Talking Textures

Designed to appeal to the senses, the inventive array of textures here will complement any outfit as well as becoming a talking point. Use your favourite pasta shapes to make into a piece of jewellery, spray paint foam, add gilt studs or tear paper for a wild look.

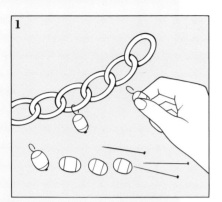

1 *To make the chain bracelet, use wire cutters to cut a 19cm (7³/4in) length of thick chain. Fix six black and white glass beads to headpins following the Using A Headpin technique on page 23. Fix to the chain links. Follow the Fixing A Boltring Fastening on page 22 to fasten the bracelet.*

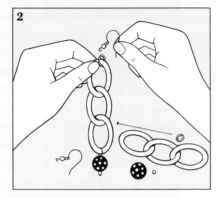

2 *Use wire cutters to cut two lengths of three links of thick chain for the drop earrings. Paint black beads with white spots using craft paints, leave to dry then fix to headpins with a small white bead following the Using A Headpin technique on page 23. Fix to one end of the chain. Fix a large jumpring to the other end and fix to an earring wire.*

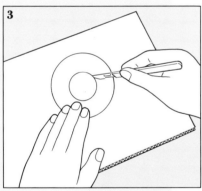

3 *The armlet, bangle and pendant are made from papier mâché. You will need a suitable mould for the armlet and bangle such as a 6.5cm (2⅝in) diameter straight sided container. Smear the mould with petroleum jelly which will act as a releasing agent. Cut a 7.5 cm (3in) diameter circle of corrugated card for the pendant. Cut a 3cm (1¹/4in) diameter hole in the centre using a craft knife.*

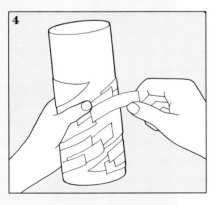

4 *Cut a cardboard kitchen roll tube to 15cm (6in) tall. Cut along the seam for the armlet. Slip the armlet over the mould to stretch it open. Tear newspaper into strips 8mm (⁵/16in) to 2cm (³/4in) wide. Mix PVA medium with a little water to thin it. Brush the solution onto strips. Apply eight layers to the armlet, overlapping the cardboard edges. Apply 15 layers around the mould for the bangle for a depth of 8cm (3¹/4in). Apply 2 layers to the pendant.*

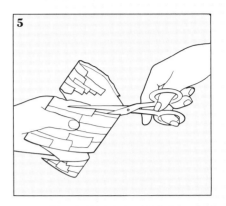

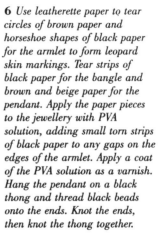

5 *Leave to dry, then remove the armlet and bangle from the moulds. Cut the papier mâché edges level with the cardboard on the armlet. Apply two layers of papier mâché to the inside, then trim the edges level. Trim the bangle edges level. Apply a final layer of papier mâché using leatherette paper – use beige for the armlet, white for the bangle and black for the pendant.*

6 *Use leatherette paper to tear circles of brown paper and horseshoe shapes of black paper for the armlet to form leopard skin markings. Tear strips of black paper for the bangle and brown and beige paper for the pendant. Apply the paper pieces to the jewellery with PVA solution, adding small torn strips of black paper to any gaps on the edges of the armlet. Apply a coat of the PVA solution as a varnish. Hang the pendant on a black thong and thread black beads onto the ends. Knot the ends, then knot the thong together.*

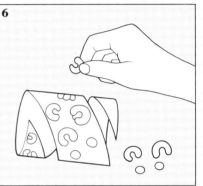

7 *To make the stud earrings, cut a 2.5cm (1in) square of thick card. Cover with crocodile skin effect paper. Fix a stud to the centre. Super glue a clip-on earring back to the back of each earring.*

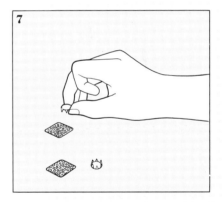

8 *To add texture to three brown oval beads for the necklace, cut tiny fragments of black paper. Insert the beads onto cocktail sticks and brush with PVA medium. Press the paper fragments to the beads using tweezers. Leave to dry then apply a final coat of PVA medium as a varnish. Thread onto a brown thong with three black beads on either side. Thread two black beads onto ends. Knot the ends then knot the thong together.*

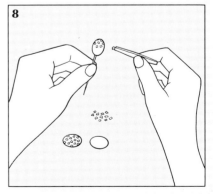

*Have a wild time wearing
se animal print accessories.
e dramatic effects are created
h papier mâché and animal
n papers.*

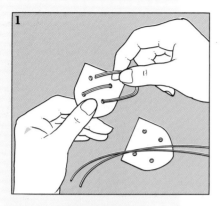

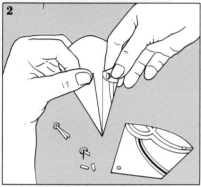

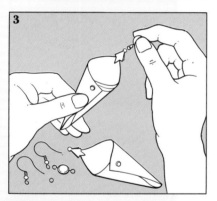

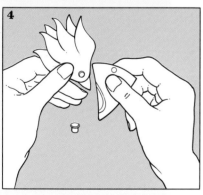

1 To make the shield earrings, cut two shields from thin copper sheet (available from craft shops). Pierce four holes in the shields, marking the corners of a rectangle on the centre. Thread two lengths of fine silver wire through the holes, making a cross on the front. Super glue the wire ends to the back. Pierce a hole at the top of the shield, fix to a jumpring.

2 To make the blue earrings, use at the template on page 102 to cut a pair of flasks from a printed metal drink can using old scissors. Make a 4mm (³/₁₆in) diameter hole at the dots. Cut the prongs of a brass paper fastener to 6mm (¹/₄in) long. Overlap the flask edges matching the holes. Insert the paper fastener through the holes, splay the prongs open on the inside. Pierce a hole at the cross with a thick needle. Fix a pendant holder to the hole.

3 Thread a bead onto wire to finish the shield and blue flask earrings. Make a loop at each end following the Pinning Beads technique on page 23. Fix to the top of the earring. Fix to a jumpring then to an earring wire.

4 To make the torch brooch, use the templates on page 102 to cut one front flame and one back flame from a reddish printed metal drink can. Cut a torch from a dark printed metal drink can. Make a 6mm (¹/₄in) hole at the dots. Matching the holes, position the front flame on the back flame and then the torch on top. Fix together with an eyelet through the holes. Bend the flanges outwards. Bind bonsai wire around the torch, super glue the ends to the back. Super glue a brooch pin to the back.

5 *To make the blue necklace, cut four shields and one pennant from printed metal drinks cans using old scissors. Snip off any sharp points. Pierce a hole at the top and fix to a pendant holder. Fix to a small jumpring. Bend the shields and pennant between your fingers to curve them. Make up the necklace following the Making A Necklace technique on page 22, alternating cylindrical blue beads with metallic discs and placing shields and pennant at the centre.*

6 *Bend bonsai wire into a spiralled 'S' shape for the pendant. Thread onto a thong, follow the Fixing Endclamps technique on page 22 to fasten the pendant. To make the copper bracelet, cut two strips of thin copper sheet 30 x 1.2cm (11³/4 x ¹/2in). Position one end of a strip on the other at right angles and super glue together.*

7 *Bend the lower strip up and fold it over the other then fold the next strip over the top. Continue folding the strips in this way then super glue the overlapped ends together. Cut off any excess. Make another concertina copper length in the same way. Pierce a hole in the centre of the ends. Thread a headpin through the hole from the underside.*

8 *Thread a metallic bead and small copper coloured disc onto each headpin. Make a loop in the headpin following the Using A Headpin technique on page 23. Fix the loops of the end two concertina lengths together. Fasten the other ends following the Fixing A Boltring Fastening technique on page 22.*

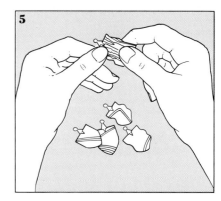

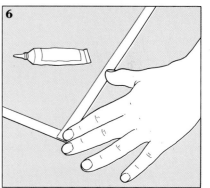

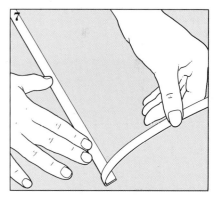

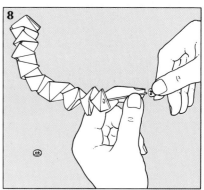

57

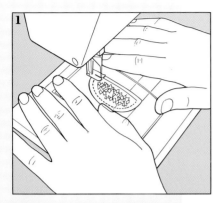

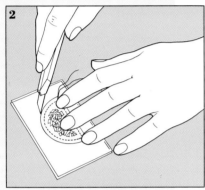

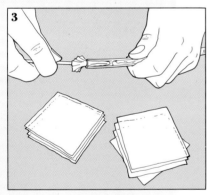

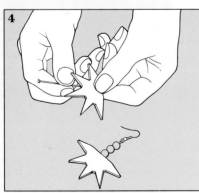

1 *To make the trapped sequin earrings place acetate over the half circle template on page 102 and trace around the lines with a chinagraph pencil. Cut out a square leaving at least 2cm (⁵/8in) all round the shape. Cut two acetate backing squares the same size and machine around the inner curved line using a polyester thread. Stuff with glitter and cut up sequins, then machine the inner straight line. Pull threads to the back and tie a knot, trim and apply a dab of glue to hold.*

2 *Cut out earrings on the outer line. Glue earring findings to the back using a transparent glue.*

3 *To make the plastic tube earrings, cut two pieces of plastic tube 6.5cm (2¹/2in) in length. Using a hot darning needle pierce two holes for the earring fixings at one end of each tube. Cut six squares each of brightly coloured twinkle organza in two colours. Fold into small squares and using a knitting needle push squares into the tube alternating colours. Leave one colour sticking out and secure with a dab of glue. Make a wire triangle and attach earring wires. The bangle is made from two thicknesses of plastic tube. Firstly measure your wrist, then cut two pieces of tube making sure the smaller one will fit inside the thicker piece. Fill the thicker piece with organza squares and the smaller one with glitter, then insert the smaller tube into the larger one and stick with clear glue.*

4 *For the foam earrings, trace the template on page 102 onto thin foam. Cut out two earring shapes with a sharp knife, then place them in a spray booth. Spray paint leaving to dry between coats. Hold the pieces down with a pin so they do not blow away. Once the paint is dry, thread a headpin through the foam, add three beads, then make a loop and attach earring wires.*

▶ *Simple touches make these special pieces of jewellery wonderful. Acetate can be bought in most craft stores.*

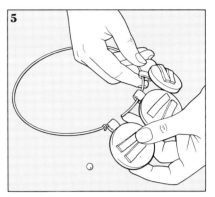

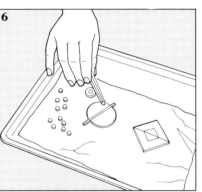

5 *For the foam necklace, cut two circles 4cm (1¹/2in) and one circle 4.5cm (1³/4in) in diameter from 6cm (¹/4in) foam, plus eleven narrow strips. Using a spray booth, spray the shapes with car paint holding them down with a pin. Leave to dry between coats. Glue strips onto the circles with a clear glue, then add back strips to hold the circles together. Make foam loops for the gold necklet to go through.*

6 *To make the plastic brooch, make a template from a circle or square and cut in half. Cut out the shape in hot water plastic using different colours for each half, then punch several dots from each colour and cut a couple of narrow strips to fit between the shapes. Heat the oven to 200°C/400°F/Gas Mark 6 and arrange the brooch pieces onto a baking sheet. They will fuse after a couple of minutes. Allow to cool, add the beads then glue a brooch clip onto the back.*

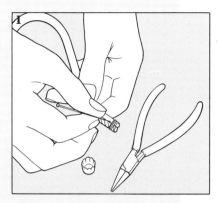

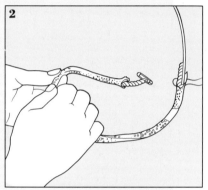

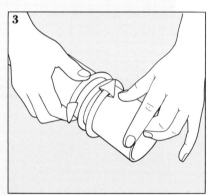

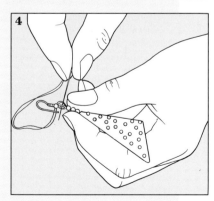

1 *To make the red and gold necklace, make a rouleau tube from red silky fabric 70 x 3cm (27$\frac{1}{2}$ x 1$\frac{1}{4}$in) following the Making A Rouleau Tube technique on page 17. Thread the tube with cotton cord size 6 and wind 1m (39in) of thick gold cord around it. Hold the necklace ends in place with a pin and tie a single knot in the centre. Carefully remove pins, trim ends and glue to stop the cord unravelling. Wind thread around the ends and finish with a bellcap, headpin and clasp.*

2 *To make the spiral bangle, cut out a strip of fabric on the bias, 56 x 4cm (22 x 1$\frac{1}{2}$in) following instructions for Making A Rouleau Tube Technique on page 17. Cut a piece of cotton cord and thick bonsai wire to the same length. Wrap tape around the ends of the cord to stop it unravelling. Thread the cord and wire through.*

3 *Trim tube ends and glue to hold. Cut four leather triangles and glue over the ends. When dry wind the bangle around a cardboard tube to get a spiral.*

4 *To make the yellow and red earrings, draw around the template on page 102 and cut out twice in stiff interfacing, twice in thin wadding and twice in red leather or another non fraying material. Cut out two yellow silk shapes approximately 6mm ($\frac{1}{4}$in) wider all round. Check you have a left and a right, then wrap the silk around the wadding and stiff interfacing holding it in place with fabric glue. When dry, sew on beads then glue on leather backs. Sew findings on with polyester thread, passing the thread through three beads and over the finding loop, then back through the beads. Before stitching securely, check the fixing faces the correct way.*

5 *To make the red silk bangle, draw an outer circle on paper 11cm (4¹/4in) in diameter and an inner circle wide enough for your hand. Transfer this template to a piece of red silk. Draw some geometric shapes onto fusible interfacing and put onto scraps of coloured silk. Attach shapes to circle following the Fusible Interfacing technique on page 19. Place thin paper under the silk circle and machine sew random lines with gold thread. Knot the threads on the back and tear away the paper. Place a second piece of red silk behind and sew around the inner and outer circle with a straight stitch using a matching thread. Then work a close satin stitch just outside the sewn lines. Cut the bangle out carefully, trimming close to the satin stitch.*

6 *Make a slit through the back fabric and stuff with wadding. Close by sewing a patch of coloured silk over the opening.*

7 *To make the frame brooch, draw a 5cm (2in) square on a piece of Haboutai silk and fit it inside a small embroidery frame. Use gold gutta to outline the square, then draw wavy lines across the square. Once dry, paint between the gutta lines with silk paint. Steam fix the paint on the wrong side when dry. Cut around the square outside the gutta outline. Cut a 10cm (4in) square from non-fraying gold fabric and draw two lines diagonally on the reverse of the fabric. Mark a 7.5cm (3in) square and a 3cm (1¹/4in) inner square. Using a craft knife cut out the inner square and four 1cm (¹/4in) squares at each corner of the gold fabric. Place frame over the silk square and hold in place with glue. Cut a piece of thin wadding 7.5cm (3in), and place this behind the picture. Machine appliqué with satin stitch around the aperture. Straight stitch mitred corners on the frame. Cut a piece of card 7.5cm (3in)*

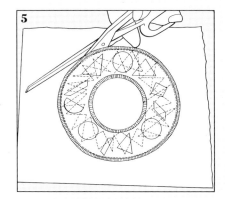

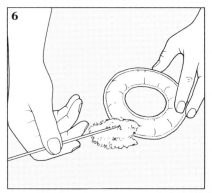

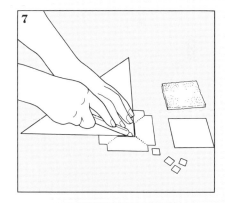

square and place it behind the frame. Wrap the excess fabric around it holding in place with fabric glue. Back the frame with a piece of card and glue on a brooch pin.

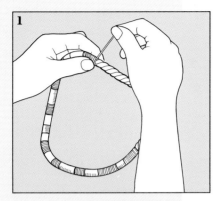

1 *Cut a 46cm (18in) length of thick upholstery cord, and bind the ends with PVA glue. Cut five 76cm (30in) lengths of both silver crochet yarn and pale pink cotton perle No. 5. Cut four 46cm (18in) lengths in both blue and bright pink perle, plus four 61cm (24in) lengths in dark turquoise perle. Starting and finishing with a dab of glue, bind cord with threads butting each thread up to the next. When the cord is covered attach bell caps at ends.*

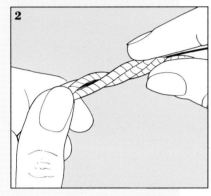

2 *To make the wire bangle, cut a 50cm (20in) length of soft dressing gown cord. To stop the cord unravelling, bind the ends with fabric glue. Insert medium-weight bonsai wire into the cord twisting as you work. Cut the wire end and tuck into the cord.*

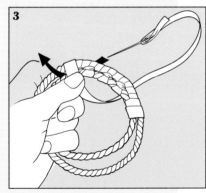

3 *Bend the cord to fit in a double circle over your hand. Cut a length of narrow satin ribbon 111cm (44in) and start to wind around both cords holding the first twist with a couple of stitches. Wrap two twists over the outside circle and one over the inside circle, passing the ribbon over the longer wrap to make a knot.*

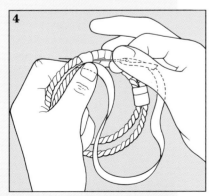

4 *Pass the ribbon from the back over the longer wrap, then through to the back before continuing with two wraps over the outside cord. Carry on making stitches until you have covered the circle. Cut the ribbon and finish with a couple of stitches. Twist end of bangle using a pair of bull nosed pliers.*

5 For the pink brooch, cut a piece of stiff interfacing and backing card in an oval 5cm (2in) long, also cut a piece of string. Glue string to interfacing. Following the Free Machine Embroidery technique on page 16 and setting zig-zag to widest measure, stitch the string to cover it. Turn the machine to straight stitch and fill in the background. Trim threads, then glue card and brooch pin to back.

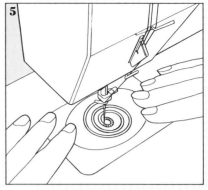

6 For the bound earrings, follow the Free Machine Embroidery technique on page 16, setting the zig-zag to the widest measure. Fit the darning foot. Place a brass ring under the darning foot and sew around the ring until it is totally covered. Tie the threads securely. Cover four large and two smaller rings, thread together using silver beads to separate the rings. Attach earring wires. This technique is used to bind cords.

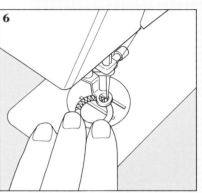

7 The bracelet is made in the same way as the bound earrings. Cover four large and five small rings with machine embroidery thread. Decorate large rings by making a pinwheel with silver thread. Start with a knot take the thread across the ring and back again, twisting the thread each time it crosses the centre. Make the bracelet by joining the rings and adding silver beads between each one. Finish with a boltring.

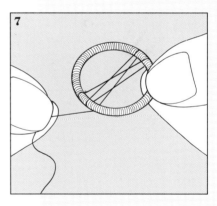

◀ *Cords of all shapes and sizes make amazing pieces of jewellery, and they are so easy to fashion. Simply add a couple of stitches to hold the cords and hey presto a wonderful new brooch.*

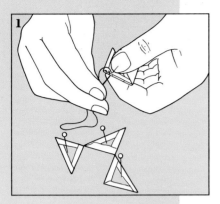

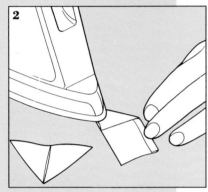

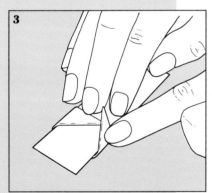

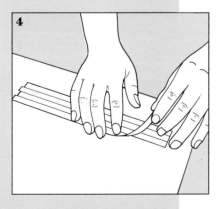

1 *To make the star brooch, trace the template on page 102 and cut out shapes in stiff interfacing. Cut out all silk shapes 6mm (¹/4in) larger than the templates. Place the interfacing over the silk shapes and pin to a polystyrene tile. Then following the Wrapping Fabric to the Back technique on page 19 wrap the silk over the interfacing. Once dry, sew the triangles around the centre square using small stitches. Cut a backing star from card and paint. Glue to the back and finally add a brooch pin. The three dimensional brooch is made in the same way but uses light, medium and dark fabrics and the sequin star and bead are added before attaching the back and brooch pin.*

2 *To make triangle bangle, trace the template on page 102. Attach fusible interfacing onto both orange and green fabric. Leave the backing paper on and using the template, cut out six orange and six green shapes. Fold shapes and press in the creases, remove backing paper and repress. The triangles should stick firmly.*

3 *Cut a band of stiff interfacing, 20 x 3cm (8 x 1¹/4in) and using fabric paint and a toothbrush splatter the band. Paint a 1.5cm (¹/2in) band of PVA glue on the back base of the triangles and leave to dry. Position the first triangle onto the right side and iron in position. Turn over and iron one flap over another. Position the next triangle and repeat until the band is covered. Trim band so the first triangle overlaps last, then add touch and close tape for a fastening.*

4 *To make the patchwork brooch, cut strips of coloured paper 30 x 1cm (12 x ¹/2in) in width. Hold the tops of the paper strips with masking tape and spray the backs with glue. Using cartridge paper, rule two guide lines 10cm (4in) apart. Attach strips to the guide lines.*

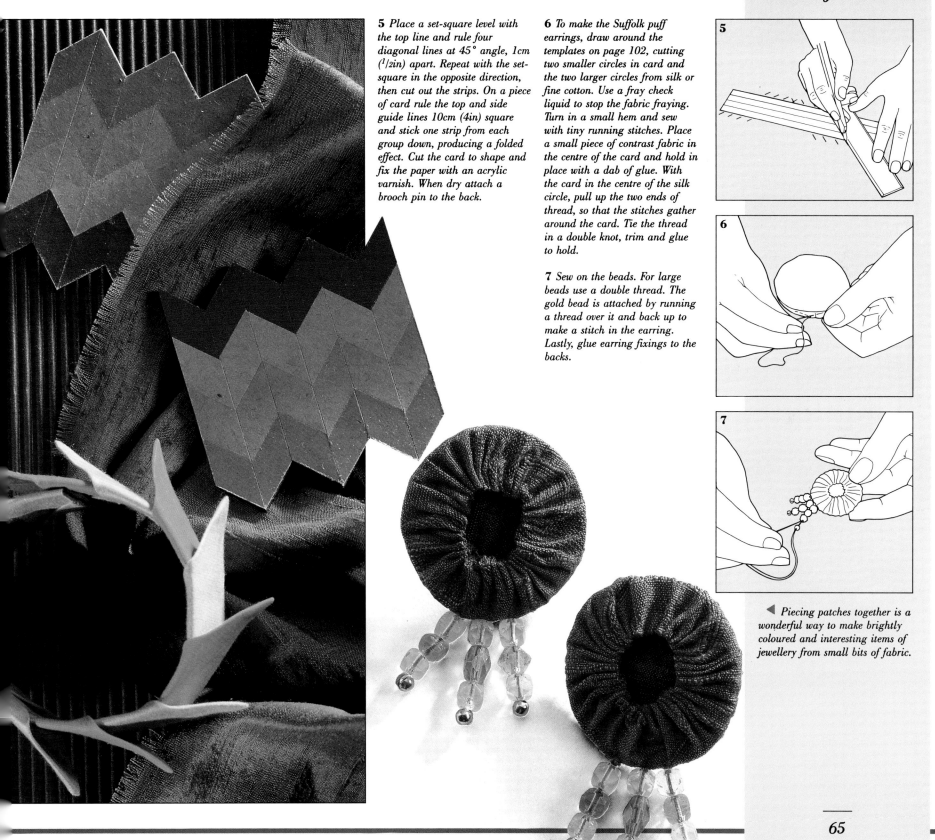

5 *Place a set-square level with the top line and rule four diagonal lines at 45° angle, 1cm (¹/₂in) apart. Repeat with the set-square in the opposite direction, then cut out the strips. On a piece of card rule the top and side guide lines 10cm (4in) square and stick one strip from each group down, producing a folded effect. Cut the card to shape and fix the paper with an acrylic varnish. When dry attach a brooch pin to the back.*

6 *To make the Suffolk puff earrings, draw around the templates on page 102, cutting two smaller circles in card and the two larger circles from silk or fine cotton. Use a fray check liquid to stop the fabric fraying. Turn in a small hem and sew with tiny running stitches. Place a small piece of contrast fabric in the centre of the card and hold in place with a dab of glue. With the card in the centre of the silk circle, pull up the two ends of thread, so that the stitches gather around the card. Tie the thread in a double knot, trim and glue to hold.*

7 *Sew on the beads. For large beads use a double thread. The gold bead is attached by running a thread over it and back up to make a stitch in the earring. Lastly, glue earring fixings to the backs.*

◀ *Piecing patches together is a wonderful way to make brightly coloured and interesting items of jewellery from small bits of fabric.*

Funky Junk

It's amazing what you can make into jewellery. Here unusual items from nuts and bolts to real sweets have been turned into something special to wear. Perhaps the hardware store, refuse tip or the local junk shop are worth another visit with your jewellery-making in mind.

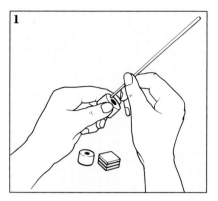

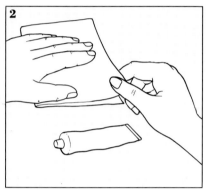

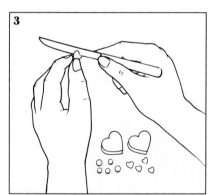

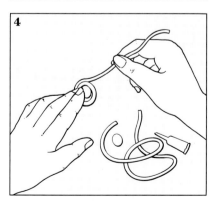

1 *To make an edible necklace of licorice sweets, pierce a hole through each sweet with a skewer. If you wish to lengthen the life of the necklace, apply ten coats of satin varnish. Use a small paintbrush to apply varnish into the holes. Remember that a varnished necklace cannot be eaten. Make up the necklace with black semi-circular beads between the sweets and small black beads at each end following the Making A Necklace technique on page 22.*

2 *Stick two layers of felt together with fabric glue to make the felt heart necklace. Use the template on page 103 to cut twenty-four hearts in four colours. Make up the necklace with coloured wooden beads in various shapes between the hearts and at each end following the Making A Necklace technique on page 22.*

3 *The heart cufflinks and flower ring are made from plastic clay that hardens in the oven. Roll the clay out flat 6mm (¹/₄in) thick. Use the templates on page 103 to cut two hearts and a flower. Roll small balls of contrasting coloured clay for the tiny hearts. Squeeze one side to a point and indent the top with a knife. Press to the large hearts. Roll a ball of contrasting coloured clay and press to the flower centre. Bake the pieces following the clay manufacturer's instructions. Leave to cool, then gloss varnish the flower. Glue to the cufflink and ring backs using a glue recommended by the clay manufacturer.*

4 *To make the round earrings, cut the end of a black thong diagonally. Glue around a jewellery stone with super glue. Cut the end diagonally. Glue a clip-on earring back to the earring back with super glue.*

5 *To make the drop earrings, roll out flat 6mm (¹/4in) thick pink, yellow and lemon coloured clay that hardens in the oven . Use the templates on page 103 to cut two flowers from pink clay, two hearts from yellow clay and two hearts from lemon clay. Pierce a hole at the dots and the point of the yellow heart with a needle.*

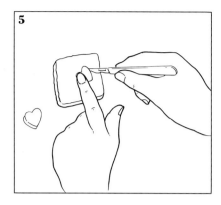

6 *Bake the flowers and hearts following the manufacturer's instructions. Allow to cool, then gloss varnish the pieces. Fix a pendant holder to each hole then fix together with jumprings. Stick a clip-on earring back to the back of the flowers using glue recommended by the clay manufacturer.*

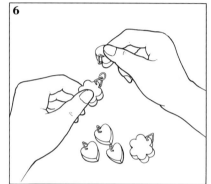

7 *The beads for the bracelet are made from plastic clay that hardens in the oven. To make cylindrical beads, roll a 8mm (⁵/16in) wide sausage of clay. Roll a contrasting coloured clay out flat 2mm (¹/16in) thick and wrap around the sausage. Roll the sausage to narrow it then cut into 1cm (³/8in) slices. To make square beads, roll clay out flat 6mm (¹/4in) thick. Press two colours together and cut into squares. You will need approximately fifty-four beads.*

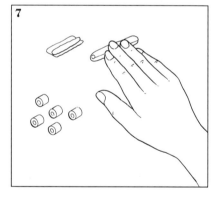

8 *Bend wire into a small loop with a pair of round nosed pliers. Cut off the excess wire leaving a 1cm (³/8in) stalk. Insert the stalk into a cut edge of the cylindrical beads and corner of the squares. Bake the beads in the oven following the clay manufacturer's instructions. Make up the bracelet with two rocaille beads between each clay bead, following the Fixing A Boltring technique on page 22.*

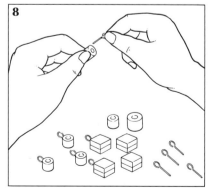

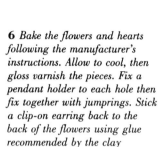
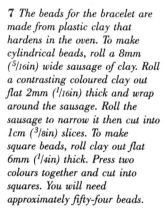

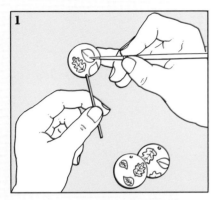

1 *To make the painted bead necklace, insert cocktail sticks into wooden beads for painting. If the bead holes are large, wrap cling film (plastic wrap) around the end of the stick to flatten it. Paint with craft paints, use a fine paintbrush to add leaf motifs and dots in bright colours. Thread onto a thong. Fasten the ends following the Fixing Endclamps technique on page 22.*

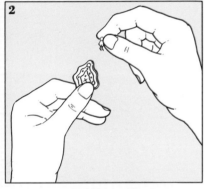

2 *To make the pink pearl necklace, use the templates on page 103 to cut two four-sided stars, two small diamonds, two large beach leaves and one large diamond from mounting board. Paint with pearlized craft paint, then varnish. Pierce a hole at the top and hang on a pendant holder. Fix to a large jumpring. Make up a necklace of pink pearls, arranging the hanging components in the centre, following the Making A Necklace technique on page 22.*

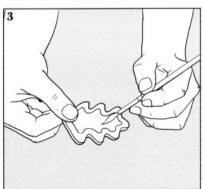

3 *For the oak leaf brooch, use the template on page 103 to cut a small and large oak leaf and a four-sided star from mounting board. Carefully cut out veins. Paint the large leaf green with yellow in the centre where it will show through the veins. Paint the small leaf red and star turquoise.*

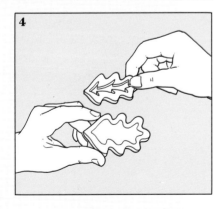

4 *Super glue the small leaf on the large leaf and coat with varnish. Pierce a hole on two opposite points on the star and at the dot on the leaf. Fix a large jumpring to the leaf and lower point on the star. Fix a pendant holder to the jumprings. Fix the upper hole on the star to the leaf pendant holder. Fix a drop bead to the remaining pendant holder.*

▶ *Offcuts of thick card are the main materials used for this bold collection of brightly painted jewellery. Craft and poster paints are perfect for the job.*

5 *Use the templates on page 103 to cut two small and two large beech leaves and two four-sided stars from mounting board for the leaf earrings. Carefully cut out the veins. Paint the large leaves red with yellow in the centre where it will show through the veins. Paint the small leaves turquoise and the stars yellow. Super glue the small leaves on the large leaves. Coat with varnish. Pierce a hole at the top of the outer leaves and two opposite corners on the stars.*

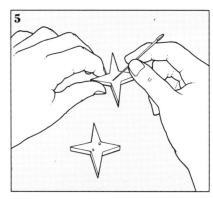

6 *Fix large jumprings to the holes on the stars. Thread two 1cm (³/8in) diameter beads onto wires, make a loop at each end following the Pinning Beads technique on page 23. Fix to a jumpring on the stars then onto earring wires. Fix the leaves to the lower jumpring on the stars with a pendant holder.*

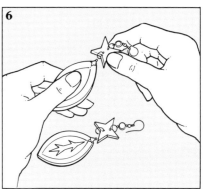

7 *To make the stickpin, use the templates on page 103 to cut a vase and six vase leaves from mounting board. Paint the pieces, painting simple motifs on the vase and veins on the leaves. Varnish the pieces. Super glue lengths of thick silver wire to the back of the leaves. Arrange the leaves above the vase, then super glue the wires to the back of the vase. Super glue a stickpin behind the vase.*

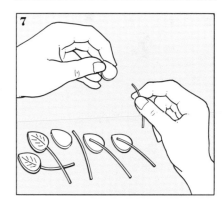

8 *To make the diamond shaped earrings, use the template on page 103 to cut two large diamonds and two small diamonds from mounting board. Cut out the stars on the small diamonds. Paint with pearlized paints, painting the large diamond pink with lilac in the centre where it will show through the star. Paint the small diamond green. Super glue the small diamond on the large diamond. Paint finer details, then varnish. Super glue a clip-on earring back to the back.*

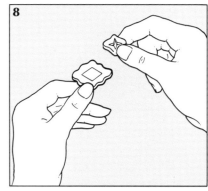

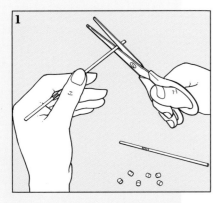

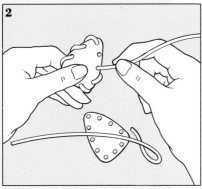

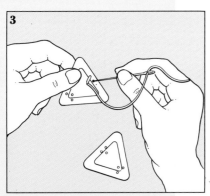

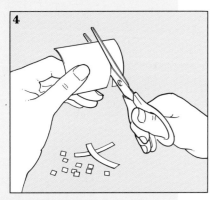

1 *To make the necklace, cut coloured plastic flexible drinking straws into slices approximately 1cm (³/8in) wide. Thread onto a thong, fastening the ends following the Fixing Endclamps technique on page 22.*

2 *To make the lace edged earrings, cut teardrop shapes from a printed waxed cardboard fruit juice carton. Pierce holes around the edges and lace with a plastic thong. Stick the thong to the back of the earrings with craft glue. Thread a plastic bead onto wire, then make loops at each end following the Pinning Beads technique on page 23. Fix the lower loop to the top hole on the earring. Fix the other loop to a plastic earring wire.*

3 *To make the triangular clip-on earrings, use the template on page 104 to cut two large and two small triangles from a printed waxed cardboard fruit juice carton. Stick together with craft glue. Pierce a hole at the dots, sew the triangles together with embroidery thread. Stick earring backs to the back of the triangles with craft glue.*

4 *Cut a coloured plastic bottle into squares for the bracelet. Pierce a hole through the centre of each square. Make up the bracelet following the Fixing A Boltring Fastening technique on page 22, threading the squares between plastic beads.*

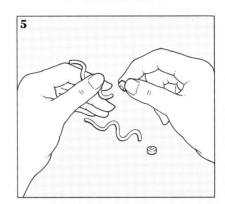

5 *Bend red plastic covered wire into curves for the squiggle earrings. Push a plastic bead with a large hole onto one end. Stick in position with craft glue. Paint the bead and end of the wire with green craft paint. Pierce a hole through the top of the plastic covered wire and fix to a pendant holder. Fix to a plastic earring wire.*

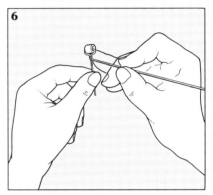

6 *Use the template on page 104 to cut a windmill from a printed waxed cardboard fruit juice carton for the pendant. Cut along the solid lines. Pierce a hole at the dots. Thread a plastic bead onto the centre of a 9cm (3in) length of wire. Twist the wire ends together under the bead.*

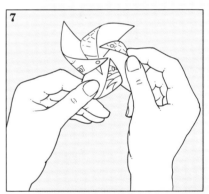

7 *Gently pull the pierced ends of the windmill between a thumb and finger to curl the ends upwards. Bend the pierced ends over the centre hole, overlapping one point on top of the next. Insert the wire ends through the holes.*

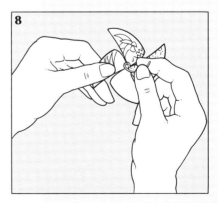

8 *Wind the wire ends into a circle on the back of the windmill to hold the shape. Thread onto a thong. Thread plastic beads onto the ends. Knot the ends then tie the thong together.*

◀ *Recycle packaging and other household goods to create colourful accessories. Waxed paper drink cartons, drinking straws and plastic bottles were used for these ingenious pieces.*

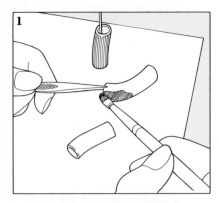

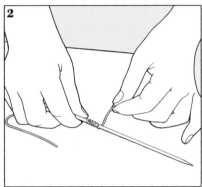

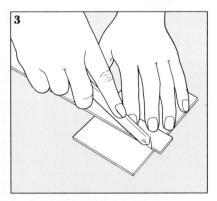

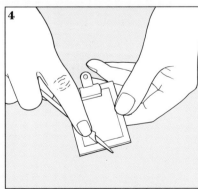

1 *To make the macaroni necklace paint seven pieces of macaroni using gouache paint, holding them with tweezers. Place on cocktail sticks stuck in a polystyrene block and leave to dry. Apply two coats. When completely dry, paint with a matt varnish. Using a puffy paint add the spots. Leave to harden overnight, then thread onto a gilt choker.*

2 *To make the paper clip earrings, cut a 10cm (4in) length of coloured wire and coil it tightly around a (3.75, No. 9) knitting needle to give a spring shape. Then bend two striped paper clips into coathanger shapes, making loops for the springs and earring attachments. Close the final bends on each spring. To make the spotted shorts, trace the template on page 104 onto card. Colour in with a felt tip pen and when dry add stationery spots. Pierce two holes in each pair of shorts and attach to the coathanger with two jumprings.*

3 *To make the clipboard brooch, spray a miniature bulldog clip red, using a spray booth, following the Using A Spray Booth technique on page 18. Cut a piece of balsa wood 5.5 x 4.5cm (2¼ x 1¾in) and rub down with fine sandpaper, then varnish. Make a small notepad from thin coloured paper, trimming it to fit, then add a tiny pencil. Shave the back of the pencil flat so that it can be glued to the paper.*

4 *Curl up a corner of the paper around the pencil. Assemble the clipboard and attach a brooch attachment to the back.*

◀ Pieces of paper, macaroni and card can be made into the most amazing items all it takes is a little knowhow.

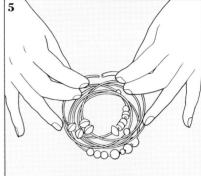

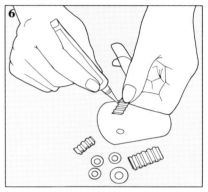

5 *To make the bead bangle, cut a 1m (36in) length of garden strimmer refill nylon and thread on a collection of interesting beads. Wind the length so that it fits over your hand, then pass each end through a curved gilt tube. This should be a firm fit so it will not need gluing.*

6 *To make the nuts and bolts brooch, draw around the template on page 101 and cut out in thin aluminium using paper scissors. Smooth any rough edges with a fine file. Gather a selection of small DIY objects, washers, plain and serrated nuts and small bolts. Using clear glue, coat the backs of the objects and press in place. Leave to dry. Spray the brooch with silver paint using a spray booth, and attach a brooch pin to the reverse.*

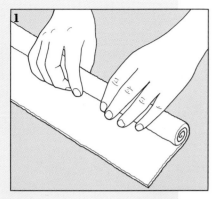

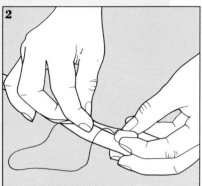

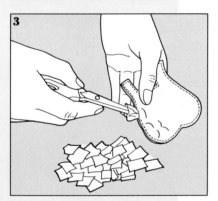

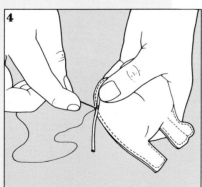

1 *To make the snake necklace, cut a bias length of thin fabric, such as a printed or dyed silk, 86 x 8cm (34 x 3in) and cut a piece of wadding to the same size. Roll the wadding firmly to make a long tube, becoming thinner at one end. Sew the wadding tightly to hold it in place. Also fold a small piece of wadding to make a triangular shape which will be the lower part of the snake's mouth. Cover this with silk. Wrap the fabric around the tube of wadding, folding under a good seam allowance. Pin then handstitch in place on what will be the underneath of the snake.*

2 *Attach the lower part of the snake's head and sew firmly in place. Overbind the snake's body with contrasting threads. Sew purl beads onto the snake's head and tail and make a fastening by sewing on a press stud.*

3 *To make the elephant brooch, draw around the template on page 104 and cut out two elephant shapes, one from felt and one from a flimsy fabric such as organdie or chiffon. Pin the two pieces of fabric together and machine stitch around the edge using a contrasting thread. Leave a gap to pad the elephant. Cut up small snippets of coloured fabric to use as a stuffing. Once padded, machine stitch the gap closed and tie off threads.*

4 *To complete the elephant, add an ear and trunk detail using the sewing machine, then attach a tusk and a tail. Add a sequin and small bead eye. Sew a brooch pin on the back.*

▶ *These heart and dice creations make a wacky combination when worn together, but will look equally good worn separately.*

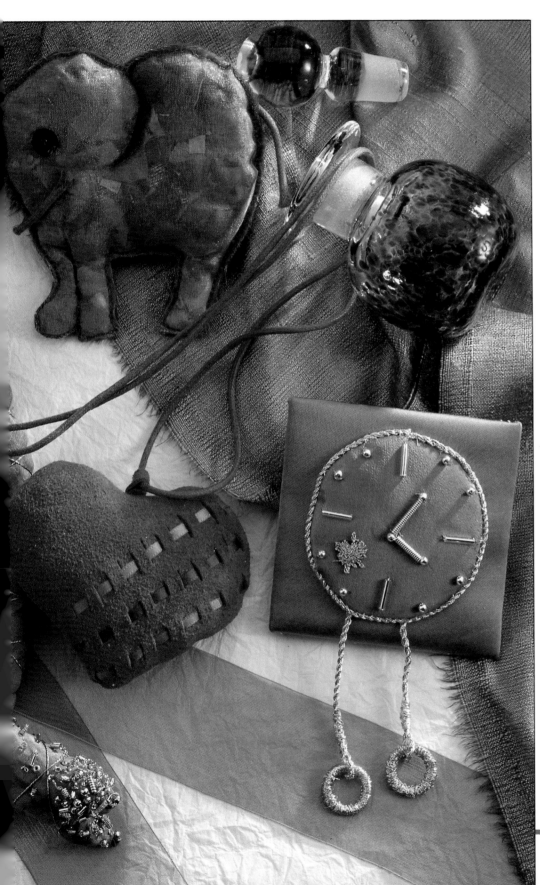

5 To make the dice earrings, cut two squares from a piece of foam rubber 2cm (³/4in) thick using a craft knife. Spray the squares with black spray paint using a spray booth, and leave to dry. Mark the numbers on the dice with white paint or beads. Complete by adding silver beads and earring findings.

6 To make the clock brooch, cut two pieces of medium weight card 7cm (2³/4in) square and one circle 5cm (2in) in diameter. Also cut one circle and one square in thin wadding. Cut three pieces of grey satin, two 9cm (3¹/2in) squares and one circle 7.5cm (3in) in diameter. Place one square of fabric over wadding on one piece of square card. Fold fabric to the back and glue, mitring the corners. Repeat for the circle, cutting V shapes out of the edges to ease fullness. Glue the last piece of fabric to the other piece of square card.

7 Sew rocailles and beads on to the clock face to show hours and hands. Attach rings to two lengths of silver cord and glue to the back of the circle. Following the Couching technique on page 21, couch a piece of silver cord to the clock face. Using fabric glue, attach the circular clock face to the padded square and leave to dry. Finally, attach the backing square and the brooch pin.

8 To make the heart pendant, draw around the template on page 104 and cut out twice in suede. Cut the slits in the suede as shown. Weave narrow ribbons through the slits and hold in place with glue. Cut a small piece of suede for the loop and place between the right sides to be stitched in. With right sides together, machine the hearts together leaving a gap for turning. Turn through, then ease out the shape. Pad with wadding then sew up the gap. Thread a cord through the loop and tie.

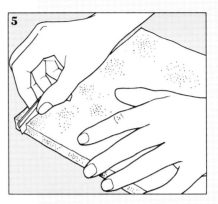

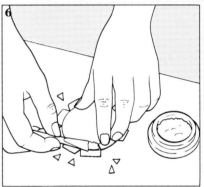

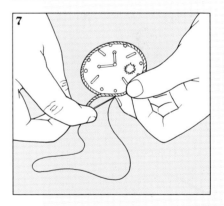

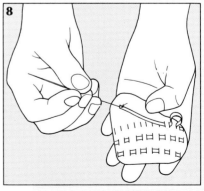

Funky Junk

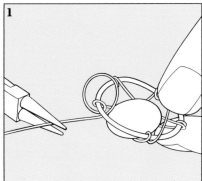

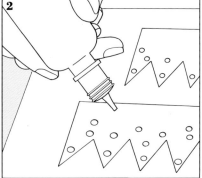

▶ *Wire springs and car spray paint may not seem very attractive in their own right, but added together they make wonderful pieces of jewellery.*

1 *To make the wire wrapped pendant, cut a length of thick bonsai wire 10cm (4in) long and form into a rough circle, butting the ends. Cut a second length of fine bonsai wire 30cm (12in) and wrap around the wire circle back and forth holding the glass stone in place. Wind the ends of the wire tightly to close. Tie a satin ribbon over the join in the outer circle and hold in place with a small dab of glue on the reverse.*

2 *To make the net earrings, cut two lengths of blue net 24 x 4cm (9¹/₂ x 1¹/₂in). Cut long triangles from one edge, then place the net onto a piece of baking parchment. Using glitter paint squeeze dots over the net and leave to dry overnight. Sew a small running stitch along the straight edge, then gather so that a circle forms. Tie the thread ends securely, then attach each earring to a pierced earring clip. Cover the earring centre with a large sequin and bead.*

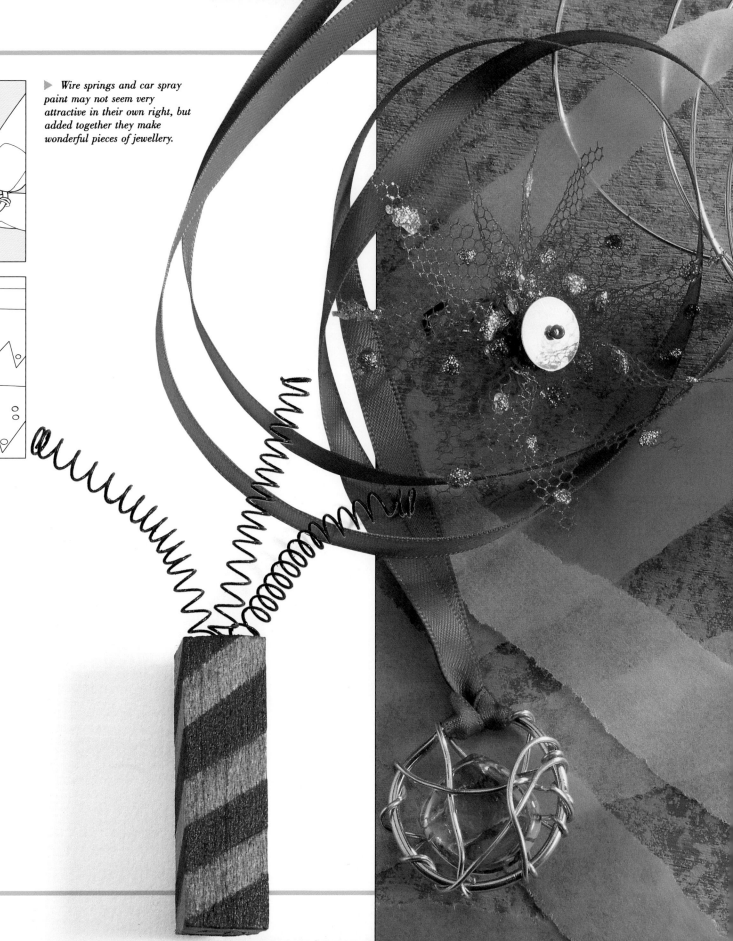

3 *To make the firework brooch, cut a length of balsa wood 4cm (1⁵/₈in) and wrap strips of masking tape around the wood, leaving areas showing. Pull three small springs straight at one end and push them into the top of the wood. Paint the brooch with spray paint following the Using A Spray Booth on page 18. Apply several coats letting each one dry first. Pull off the masking tape and add a second colour using a felt tip pen. Glue the brooch onto the fixing.*

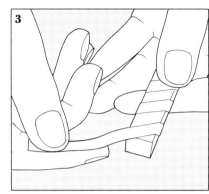

4 *To make the tissue paper earrings, cut a length of medium-weight bonsai wire and shape into a triangle, making the join halfway along one side. Cut strips of tissue paper and paint with PVA glue, before wrapping them around the shapes.*

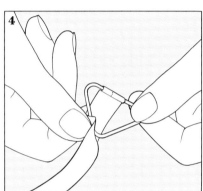

5 *Add papers until the shape is fairly thick and leave in a warm place to dry overnight. Finish decorating with torn tissue strips in contrasting colours. Attach earring fixings to finish.*

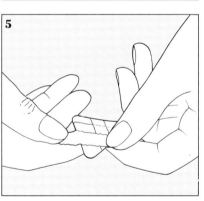

6 *To make the bead filled earrings and rings, use earring and ring blanks. Use double sided sticky tape to hold the blanks steady and carefully place seed beads in two colours in the depression of the blanks. Use an orange stick or cocktail stick to help arrange the seeds in a pattern and to keep them all upright. Once you are satisfied with the design, use the stick to drop colourless stained glass varnish into the seeds. When the beads are completely covered leave to dry overnight.*

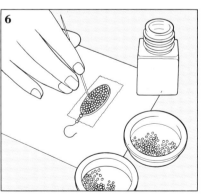

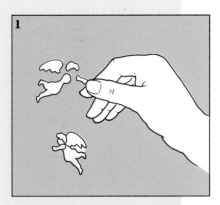

1 To make the small cherub stud earrings, use the template on page 105 to cut a pair of cherubs and arms from thin flesh-coloured foam. Cut a pair of hairdos and wings from yellow foam. Stick the arms, hairdo and wings to the cherubs with craft glue. Use a fine paintbrush to paint the facial features. Glue a flat pad ear stud to the back.

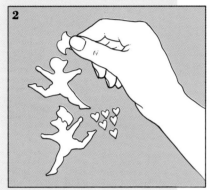

2 Use the template on page 105 to cut a pair of exotic dancers from flesh-coloured foam, a pair of hairdos from yellow foam, four small blue hearts and two small mauve hearts. Stick the hairdo in place with craft glue, then stick on the hearts as a bikini. Paint the facial features.

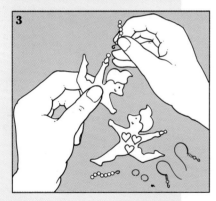

3 Fix a pendant holder to the dancer at the dots. Thread six mauve rocaille beads onto wire. Make a loop in the wire at each end following the Pinning Beads technique on page 23. Fix one end to the pendant holder. Fix the other end to a jumpring then to an earring wire.

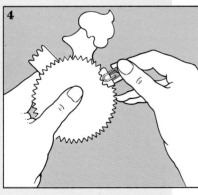

4 To make the can-can dancer brooch, cut a head, hands and legs from flesh-coloured foam. Cut the hairdo from yellow foam and shoes from blue foam. Glue the hairdo to the head and shoes to the legs with craft glue. Cut a 4.8cm (1⅞in) diameter circle of white foam with pinking shears. Glue the head behind the circle with the hands extending at each side. Bend the hands over the circle and glue in place. Hold in position with paperclips until the glue has dried. Glue the legs to the circle. Paint the facial features. Glue a brooch pin to the back.

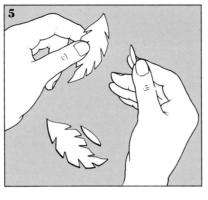

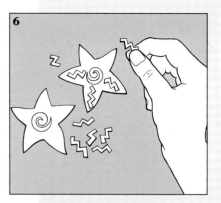

6 *To make the star clip-on earrings, use the template on page 105 to cut a pair of stars from mauve foam. Cut the spiral from yellow foam and stick to the star with craft glue. Cut narrow strips of white foam with pinking shears. Cut into short lengths and glue along each star point. Glue a clip-on earring to the back.*

5 *To make the feather earrings, use the template on page 105 to cut a pair of feathers from blue foam and slivers from red foam. Glue the foam slivers to the feathers with craft glue. Fix a pendant holder to the top, then fix to an earring wire.*

7 *To make the heart brooch, use the template on page 105 to cut a heart from red foam. Cut a smaller heart from blue foam and glue to the red heart. Cut a narrow strip of mauve foam, cutting one long edge with a craft knife and the other edge with pinking shears. Glue to the circumference of the heart. Glue a brooch pin to the back.*

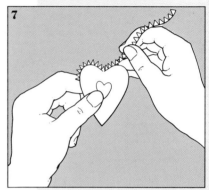

8 *To make the heart pendant, use the template on page 105 to cut a heart from red foam with pinking shears and another from blue foam with a craft knife. Cut a keyhole in the blue heart. Glue the hearts together. Fix a pendant holder to the top, fix to a large jumpring. Thread onto a thong. Cut four smaller hearts from red foam and two from blue foam. Thread onto the ends of the thonging. Knot the ends.*

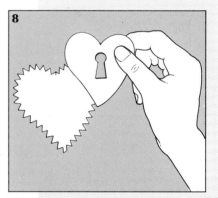

9 *To make the bracelet, cut five rectangles of blue foam 3.5 x 2.5cm (1^1/2 x 1in) with pinking shears. Cut seven small hearts from red foam, glue a heart to each rectangle. Cut narrow strips of mauve foam with pinking shears, cut into 3.5cm (1^1/2in) lengths. Glue across the hearts. Pierce a hole inside each short edge. Thread with a thong. Pierce a hole through each remaining heart, thread onto a thong and knot the ends.*

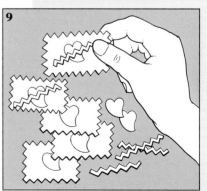

amusing selection of wacky
ery is simple to make from
oloured foam which is
able at craft shops. Cutting
am with pinking shears
an exciting serrated edge to
of the pieces.

Past Times

The inspiration for these items comes from the past, using influences from all over the world. The designs come from sources as varied as Turkish carpets, Australian Aboriginal bark paintings, Italian glass and the planets. There are rich and varied pieces, some re-using inherited materials in glamorous ways. The jewellery here is perfect for everyday and evening wear.

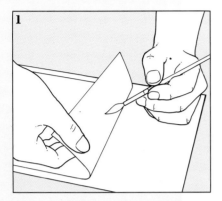

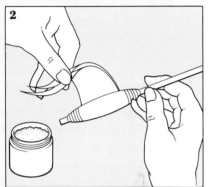

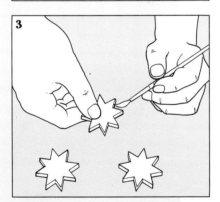

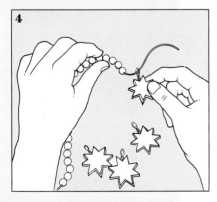

1 *To make the cocoon-shaped earrings, cut two long triangles of blue paper (the paper used here is speckled with gold and silver), the two sides measuring 71 cm (28in) with a base 6cm (2¹/₄in) wide. Cut two long triangles of gold paper, the two sides measuring 70cm (27¹/₂in) long with a base 5cm (2in) wide. Using PVA medium, stick the gold paper centrally to the wide end of the blue paper.*

2 *Wrap a length of wood dowelling with cling film (plastic wrap) to prevent paper sticking to the wood. Starting at their bases roll the triangles tightly around the dowelling, brushing with PVA as you work. Apply a final coat of PVA medium as a varnish. Leave to dry, then gently remove the dowelling. Pierce a hole through the top of the beads and fix to earring wires with a pendant holder.*

3 *To make the stars for the star earrings and bracelet, apply blue or mauve craft paint to mounting board with a sponge. Leave to dry, then dab lightly with gold craft paint. Cut out two medium and two large stars for the earrings and five small stars for the bracelet using the template on page 104. Paint the cut edges and backs with gold paint. Spray with spray varnish. Pierce a hole through one point of each star.*

4 *Dab PVA medium onto the earring stars and sprinkle with gold sequin dust. Leave to dry, then shake off excess. Fix large stars to medium stars with a pendant holder and jumpring. Super glue clip-on earring backs to the medium stars. To make a bracelet, fix pendant holders to the stars, thread gold and mauve beads and the stars onto thread. Thread on a bell cap at each end. Tie securely to a boltring and jumpring. Insert the thread back through the last six beads.*

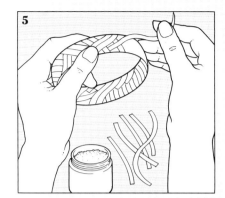

5 *Decorate a plastic bangle with torn strips of blue, mauve and turquoise tissue. Stick strips in place with PVA medium, overlapping the edges. Dab gold craft paint onto the bangle with a sponge. Cut tiny stars from gold paper using the template on page 104 and glue to the bangle. Apply two coats of PVA medium as a varnish.*

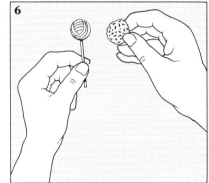

6 *To make the necklace, push nine wooden beads onto cocktail sticks to decorate them. Stick fine strips of blue, mauve and turquoise tissue to the beads with PVA medium. Leave to dry, then dab on gold craft paint with a sponge. Thread the handmade beads onto thread with gold beads at each end. Thread on a bell cap at each end. Tie thread securely to a torpedo clasp. Insert the thread back through the last six beads.*

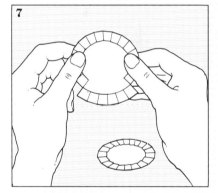

7 *To prepare the sun earrings, cut two circles of mounting board 4.5cm (1³/4 in) in diameter. Apply PVA medium to strips of torn blue mauve and turquoise tissue. Stick the strips over the circles, overlapping edges. Snip the excess tissue to the circles and stick the excess to the back.*

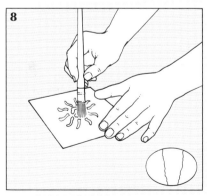

8 *To prepare the sun brooch, dab mauve paint onto mounting board with a sponge. Leave to dry, then cut a circle 5cm (2in) in diameter. Paint the cut edges with gold paint. Dab the earring and brooch circles lightly with gold craft paint using a sponge. Use the template on page 104 to draw a sun onto stencil board. Add the tiny stars for the brooch. Cut out the cutouts. Tape the stencil to the circles with masking tape and dab gold craft paint through the cutouts using a stencil brush. Remove the stencil and spray with spray varnish. Glue earclips or a brooch pin to the back.*

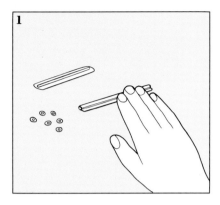

1 *The millefiore style beads are made from plastic coloured clay that hardens in the oven. To make cylindrical beads, start by rolling a 2cm (³/₄in) wide sausage of clay. To make round, oval or teardrop-shaped beads, roll balls of clay. To decorate the beads, roll fine sausages of clay. Roll a contrasting coloured clay out flat 2mm (¹/₁₆in) thick and wrap around the fine sausage. Cut 2mm (¹/₁₆in) thick slices, cut diagonally to make oval slices.*

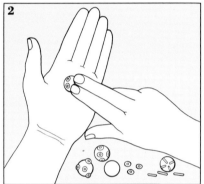

2 *Press the slices to the long sausage of clay and beads. Cut narrow strips of rolled clay and arrange on the sausage and beads. Now roll the sausage to 1.3cm (¹/₂in) wide to embed the decorations and cut into 1.5cm (⁵/₈in) cylindrical lengths. Roll the balls again until they are smooth and the decorations have been embedded. If you wish, roll the beads into oval or teardrop shapes. Pierce a hole through the beads.*

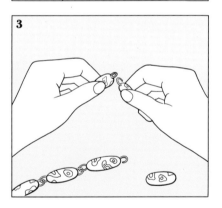

3 *Bake the beads following the clay manufacturer's instructions. Apply gloss varnish when the beads have cooled. To join the beads with wire, follow the Pinning Beads technique on page 23, then fix the ends to a clasp. Alternatively, make up necklaces following the Making A Necklace technique on page 22.*

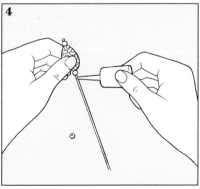

4 *To make a hatpin, thread a small gold bead, a glass bead, a large clay millefiore bead and another glass bead onto the end of a hat pin. Dab a little super glue onto the hatpin just below the last bead. Slip a small gold bead onto the hatpin and onto the glue to hold all the beads in place.*

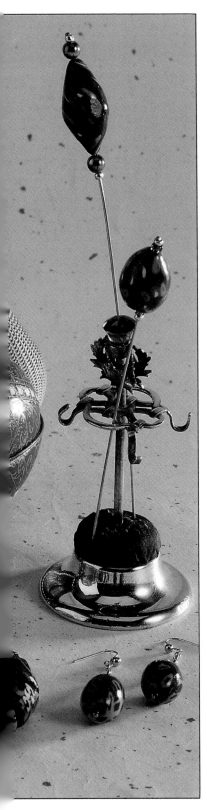

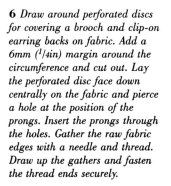

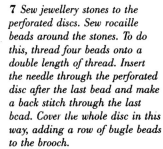

◀ *These colourful clay beads are reminiscent of beautiful Italian glass millefiore beads while the densely beaded brooch and clip-on earrings are influenced by Victorian pincushions.*

5 *To make the millefiore earrings, thread a small coloured bead, a clay millefiore bead, another small coloured bead then a small gold bead onto a headpin. Make a loop in the headpin over the last bead following the Using A Headpin technique on page 23. Fix a length of fine chain to the loop and then fix the other end to an earring wire.*

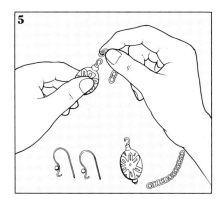

6 *Draw around perforated discs for covering a brooch and clip-on earring backs on fabric. Add a 6mm (¹/4in) margin around the circumference and cut out. Lay the perforated disc face down centrally on the fabric and pierce a hole at the position of the prongs. Insert the prongs through the holes. Gather the raw fabric edges with a needle and thread. Draw up the gathers and fasten the thread ends securely.*

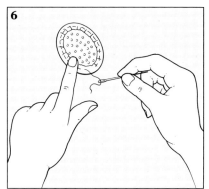

7 *Sew jewellery stones to the perforated discs. Sew rocaille beads around the stones. To do this, thread four beads onto a double length of thread. Insert the needle through the perforated disc after the last bead and make a back stitch through the last bead. Cover the whole disc in this way, adding a row of bugle beads to the brooch.*

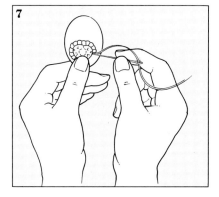

8 *To add a drop bead below the brooch, thread six beads, a drop bead and then five beads onto a double length of thread. Insert the needle back through the first bead and fasten securely to the fabric. At each side of the drop, thread a small bead, a large bead and then two more small beads onto a double length of thread. Insert the needle back through the beads, except the last. Carefully pull up the thread and fasten to the fabric. Fix the disc to the brooch or clip-on earring backs following the Fixing A Perforated Disc technique on page 20.*

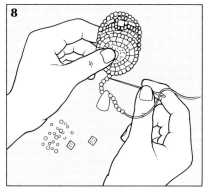

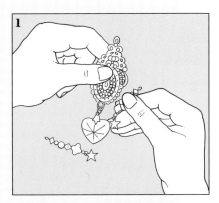

1 *To make the red heart earrings, fix a large red heart drop bead to a pendant holder and fix to a jumpring. Fix to an ornate gold earring that has filigree holes. Super glue jewellery stones to the earring. Thread beads onto two lengths of gold wire, make loops at the ends following the Pinning Beads technique on page 23. Fix a star-shaped charm to one loop, fix the other loop to the earring.*

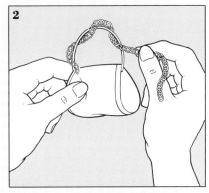

2 *To make the brooch, thread two charms onto gold wire – here, a large heart and lion were used. Super glue the wire ends to the back of a small gilt purse as a handle. Wrap the wire with fine gold chain, gluing the ends behind the purse. Super glue beads inside the purse. Glue two charms to the purse. Super glue a brooch back to the back.*

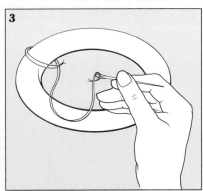

3 *To make the bangle, thread a needle with thread, knotting the ends together. Loop the threads through a plastic bangle. Bring the needle out between the threads. Pull tightly and stick the knot to the bangle with craft glue. Thread on rocaille beads, wrapping the beads around the bangle as you work.*

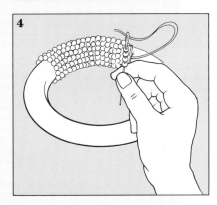

4 *If the thread runs out, cut off the needle and glue the thread ends to the bangle. Fasten a new length to the bangle in the same way as the first, close to the last bead. Thread the needle through the last four beads before threading on more beads. When the bangle is covered, part the rows of beads to glue the thread ends around the bangle.*

▶ *Broken necklaces and earrings have been dismantled and remade into this stunning collection. Simple jewellery has also been lavished with extra beads and charms to complete the extravagant effect.*

5 *The necklace has been made from a necklace of simple gold links. Fix a lion's head charm on a jumpring. If the charm has other holes, fix on smaller charms with jumprings. Fix the lion to the necklace centre. Fix red beads onto headpins following the Using A Headpin technique on page 23. Fix charms and coins onto jumprings. Fix to the links along with the headpins.*

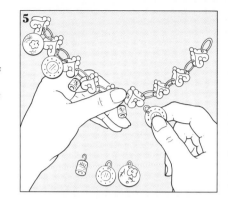

6 *To make the three-strand earrings, thread rocaille beads onto three lengths of gold wire. Add two large beads at one end. Make one length of beads 1cm ($^{3}/_{8}$in) longer than the other. Make end loops following the Pinning Beads technique on page 23. Fix to a three-hole hanger. Fix a drop bead on a pendant hanger to the long strand. Fix heart-shaped charms to the shorter strands. Thread a bead onto wire, then make loops at each end. Fix the top to a jumpring then an earring wire. Fix to the earring.*

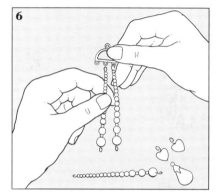

7 *To make the pearl necklace, fix gold charms onto small jumprings. Fix a pendant holder to a heart-shaped drop bead. Fix to a jumpring. Thread pearls, glass and silver beads with diamanté spacers between onto two lengths of thread, arranging the heart and charms at the centre. Make one length of beads 29cm (11$^{1}/_{2}$in) long and the other 32cm (12$^{1}/_{2}$in) long. Tie the thread ends to the holes of two two-hole hangers. Thread the threads through the last five beads. Fix to clasps or a chain fastening. Use wire cutters to cut a 20cm (8in) length of thick chain for the chain bracelet. Fix large beads onto headpins following the Using A Headpin technique on page 23. Fix large jumprings to charms and drop beads. Fix three decorations onto each chain link. Follow the Fixing A Boltring technique on page 22 to finish.*

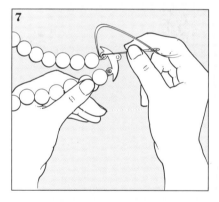

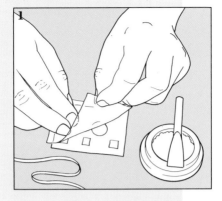

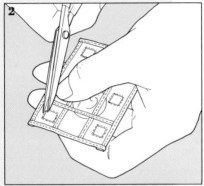

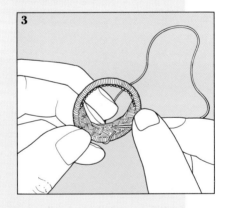

1 *To make the Art Nouveau style brooch, cut a piece of craft felt 8 x 5cm (3 x 2in) and lightly glue on six small squares of felt, a circle of felt and a length of metallic cord to form a flower (see page 105). Lay a piece of organza or other flimsy fabric over the top and machine outline, working around flower details.*

2 *Place narrow ribbons to form the frame and machine with a matching thread. Cut away the top fabrics round the felt squares to allow them to show through. Finish off the threads securely. Cut a piece of stiff card to slightly less than the brooch size and glue to the back, then add a brooch pin.*

3 *To make the ring basket earrings, sew around a curtain ring 2.5cm (1in) in diameter, using buttonhole stitch and flower thread following the Buttonhole Stitch technique on page 21.*

When complete, turn the edge of the stitching to the inside of the ring. Using a needle and thread, darn threads from one side of the ring to the other. When a firm enough fabric background has been created, cover with French knots and beads, following the Making French Knots technique on page 21. To complete the earrings, add a bead and a finding to the top of each ring and tie with a small knot.

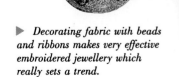

▶ *Decorating fabric with beads and ribbons makes very effective embroidered jewellery which really sets a trend.*

4 To make the choker, embroider the design in tent stitch onto 14 mesh plastic canvas following the Tent Stitch technique on page 21. Follow the colour key and chart on page 107, but omit the outer row of stitches all round the design. Use six strands of stranded cotton and a size 24 tapestry needle.

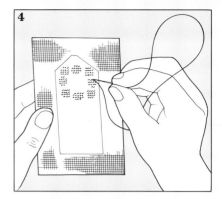

5 Start working the beaded area using two strands of thread and a size 8 crewel needle and attach one bead with every stitch. Cut out each piece leaving a margin of unworked thread of canvas all round the edge. Following the Overcast Stitch technique on page 21, finish the edges with a row of overcast stitches working with six strands of burnt sienna. Join the pieces at the points marked on the chart. Stitch a 45cm (18in) length of narrow grosgrain ribbon at each side. Neaten the back of each piece by sticking a matching piece of felt on the wrong side with fabric glue.

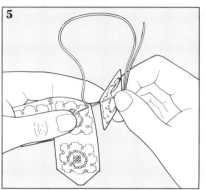

6 To make the cameo, embroider the design in back stitch following the Back Stitch technique on page 21 onto 14 count cream Aida fabric following the colour key and chart on page 107. Use two strands of stranded cotton in a size 24 tapestry needle. Press on the wrong side and mount the embroidery in a gold coloured pendant brooch.

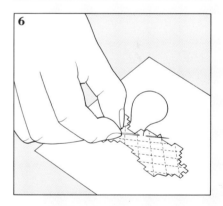

7 To make the embroidered earrings, trace the template on page 105 onto a piece of calico. Place calico into a small embroidery frame and following the Free Machine Embroidery technique on page 16, embroider the brooch, changing thread colours while you work. Change the coloured threads again to sew the background. Fasten threads and cut away excess fabric. Fold fabric edges over an oval-shaped card. Back each earring with a slightly smaller oval card and attach earring clips.

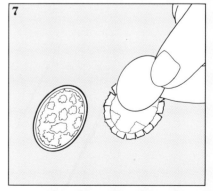

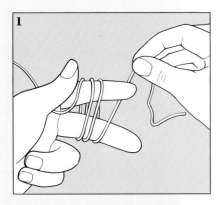

1 *To make the brooch, take an 87cm (34in) length of thick metallic thread, string or cord to make a monkey fist knot. The earrings need 69cm (27in) of finer cord each. Starting 15cm (6in) from one end, wind the cord three times around your hand from left to right.*

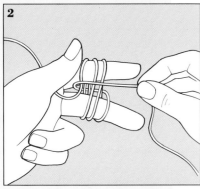

2 *Take one end and pass it horizontally around the back of your hand from right to left, returning to the right-hand side. Repeat this procedure twice, placing the cord above the previous row each time.*

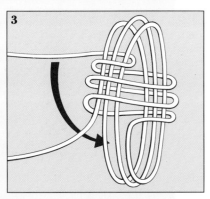

3 *Slide the cord off your hand and pass the end from the back to the front and over the strands three times.*

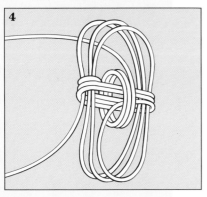

4 *Finish by taking the cord out towards the back and gently tighten to make a smooth knot. Cut and sew the ends and add a brooch pin or earring fixings.*

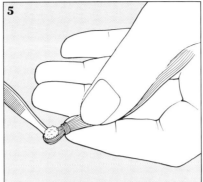

5 To make bead thread earrings, make a tassel by winding metallic thread around a 9cm (3¹/2in) card 70 times. Secure top by passing a thread through the metallic threads and tying. Pull bead over tassel to head. Stuff the head of the tassel with cotton wool. Bind tassel head and below the bead with gold thread. Attach a gold bead and earring findings to the top of the tassel, and secure the threads by tying off under the gold bead.

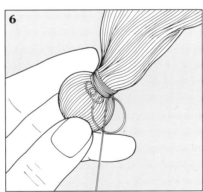

6 To make the choker, make a large tassel, using two shades of perle thread No 5. Wind the thread around an 18cm (7in) piece of card 60 times. Pad the head of the tassel with a large bead. Bind under the head of the tassel with contrasting thread. Work open buttonhole on page 21, filling in fine gold thread to cover the top part of the tassel.

7 Turn the tassel upside down and following the Buttonhole Stitch technique on page 21 work a row of ordinary buttonhole stitches over the threads holding the tassel together. Work from left to right and arrange the stitches close together. Work subsequent rows of buttonhole stitch into loops on the row above, changing the working direction after each row. You will also need to increase or decrease the number of stitches on subsequent rows to follow the shape of the tassel. When the embroidery is completed, secure the thread end neatly at the top of the tassel. Attach the tassel to a metal necklet with an eyelet.

8 The finger weave bracelet is made with two 150cm (60in) cords in contrasting colours. Tie threads together to start following the step shown.

9 Following the diagrams, weave the cords to the required length to fit your wrist. Finish one end by making a loop with cord and binding with contrasting thread. At the other end, tie an overhand knot and pull down the top loop, binding it with contrasting thread to make a knotted end.

10 To make the frizz metal earrings, make a tassel around a 5cm (2in) card following basic instructions above. When winding the threads, remember that the thickness of the tassel will depend on the size of the bell cap you are using to cover the head of the tassel. Thread a needle with a matching finer thread and knot the top of the tassel. Thread the top of the tassel into the metal cap and then through a bead. Tie the tassel and bead to the ring with a small knot, passing the thread back through the bead to end in the tassel. Finish by adding a bead and an earring wire finding to the top of the ring.

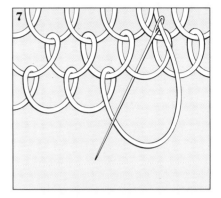

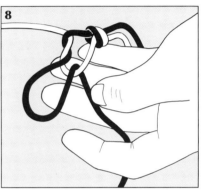

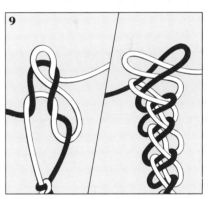

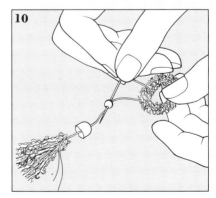

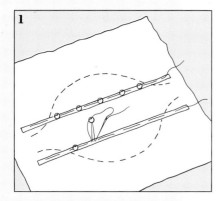

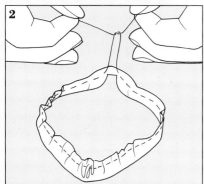

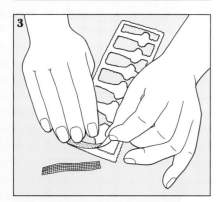

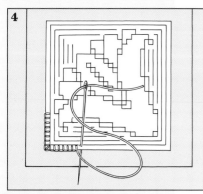

1 *To make the padded pendant, draw around the template on page 106 and cut out from card and wadding. Cut two pieces of silk 13cm (5in) square. Trace the template design onto the back of the silk and sew tacking stitches on the line. Cut two pieces of narrow turquoise ribbon and tack them in two straight lines. Attach 5 pink beads with gold thread, making a stitch on either side of the hole. Sew on sequins with turquoise beads, then add gold ribbon and blue beads.*

2 *Hold the wadding in place on the card with a small piece of double-sided tape, then run a gathering stitch around the shape just outside the original line. Cut out and gather around the wadding and card. Use the first tacked line as a guide and lace around the card on the back. Repeat for the backing side, then sew the two pieces together, leaving a gap for the gold hanging ribbon. Tuck the ribbon into the gap and sew securely.*

3 *To make the Greek machine embroidered bracelet, draw the template on page 106, measure your wrist and transfer the repeat of the design to water soluble fabric. Following the Sewing On Water Soluble Fabrics technique on page 16, sew the design. When dry, attach a strip of touch and close tape at ends.*

4 *To make the Lotus brooch, embroider the design in cross stitch and back stitch following the techniques on page 21. Use 14 count pink Aida fabric and follow the key and chart on page 107. Use two strands of stranded cotton or one strand of gold thread in a size 24 tapestry needle. Following the technique on page 21, work a row of pale pink buttonhole stitches round the design, using two strands of thread and leaving one row of unworked fabric blocks between the buttonhole stitches and the outer row of back stitch.*

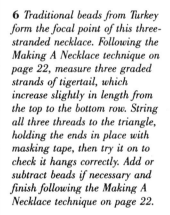

5 *Cut away the surplus fabric close to the buttonhole stitches, taking care not, to snip into the stitches. Place the embroidery right side down on a piece of polythene, then coat the back with slightly diluted PVA medium and allow to dry. Cut a piece of royal blue felt slightly larger than the brooch and attach a brooch pin at one corner. Stick the felt to the back of the embroidery with fabric glue, then trim the margin to make a neat border round the design.*

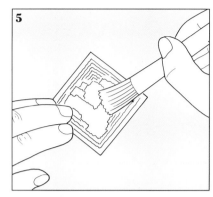

6 *Traditional beads from Turkey form the focal point of this three-stranded necklace. Following the Making A Necklace technique on page 22, measure three graded strands of tigertail, which increase slightly in length from the top to the bottom row. String all three threads to the triangle, holding the ends in place with masking tape, then try it on to check it hangs correctly. Add or subtract beads if necessary and finish following the Making A Necklace technique on page 22.*

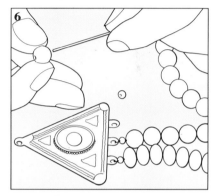

▲ *Holidays abroad provide the ideal opportunity to seek out jewellery and absorb the local culture. Traditional materials often determine the colours used, some subdued, others vivid. Markets are well worth a visit too. Here exotic beads from Greece and Turkey offer inspiration.*

7 *The fish earrings are made from silver hoops and glass fish bought in Greece. Simply thread the fish onto the hoop, then push the hoop wire firmly into the fitting to close securely. Attach a jumpring and earring wire to finish.*

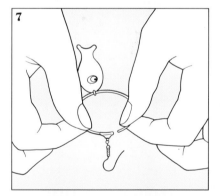

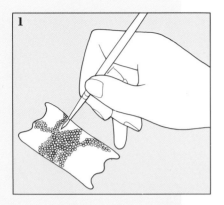

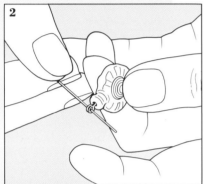

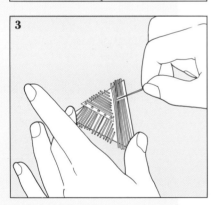

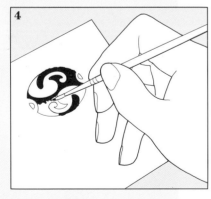

1 *The dotted pendant is made from an interesting piece of bark. Use gouache to paint rows of white and orange dots following the suggested design. Once dry, cover with a couple of coats of matt varnish. Make a jumpring, from a headpin, then drill a small hole in the bark and thread it through. Following the Making a Machine Cord technique on page 19, make a three-colour cord. Thread the cord through the jumpring.*

2 *This African inspired necklace is made from beads collected over the years. Thread the beads onto tigertail randomly, contrasting colours and textures. The dropped beads have a tiny bead and a double-looped headpin to hold them in place.*

3 *To make the collar pin, draw around the template on page 106. Place over stiff interfacing and cut out twice. Draw a centre guideline lightly in pencil on one triangle and cover with fabric glue. Following the diagram, lay pieces of cotton perle No 5 in stripes to represent paint. Stroke the thread with a pin to help it stick. Work all three colours. When they are dry, trim the edges with a sharp craft knife. Put the short length of narrow black and white spotted ribbon on first, then the longer length, followed by the three edges. Leave to dry pressed under a book. Glue the wrong side of the triangle and the backing triangle, then place a lapel pin between the two with a bead threaded at the top. Press the front and back together and place under a book to dry.*

4 *To make the Maori pendant, draw around the template on page 106 and trace onto cartridge paper. Using dark red, black and white gouache, paint the design leaving each colour to dry before starting the next. Paint two coats. Cut out the design and mount into a gilt frame following the manufacturer's instructions.*

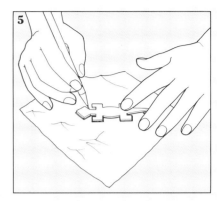

5 *To make the crocodile earrings, trace the template on page 106 onto water soluble fabric. Following the Sewing on Cold Water Soluble Fabric technique on page 16, embroider the design using special sparkly machine embroidery thread in two contrasting colours. Attach a gold bead to the crocodile and add an earring wire.*

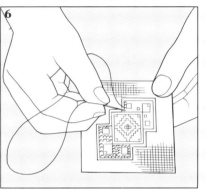

6 *Make the Turkish earrings following the Tent Stitch technique on page 21. Embroider the design in tent stitch on to 14 mesh plastic canvas following the key and chart on page 107, but omitting the outer row of stitches all round the design. Use six strands of stranded cotton in a size 24 tapestry needle. When working the beaded areas, use two strands of thread in a size 8 crewel needle and attach one bead with every stitch. Make two patterned front pieces and two plain back pieces for each pair of earrings.*

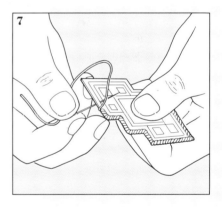

7 *Cut out each piece leaving a margin of one unworked thread of canvas all round the edge. Place the front and back pieces together with the wrong sides facing. Using six strands of dark brown thread and following the Overcasting technique on page 21, overcast the two pieces together, catching the thread in a gold jumpring at the top corner. Finally, attach a gold screw fastening to the jumpring.*

TEMPLATES AND DIAGRAMS

The following pages present the templates and patterns referred to in the projects. The templates printed in blue are reduced in size. To enlarge them draw a grid of 1.4cm (⁹⁄₁₆in) squares. Copy the design square by square using the lines as a guide. Alternatively, enlarge the templates on a photocopier to 141% (or A4 enlarged to A3). To make a complete pattern for symmetrical shapes, place the pattern on a piece of folded paper matching the 'place to fold' line to the folded edge. Cut out and open the pattern out flat to use.

CHOKER
Page 31

BRONZE CROSS BROOCH
Page 31

CROWN EARRINGS
Page 29

FLEUR-DE-LYS EARRINGS
Page 29

MACHINE EMBROIDERED BROOCH   Page 30

MACHINE EMBROIDERED EARRINGS
Page 30

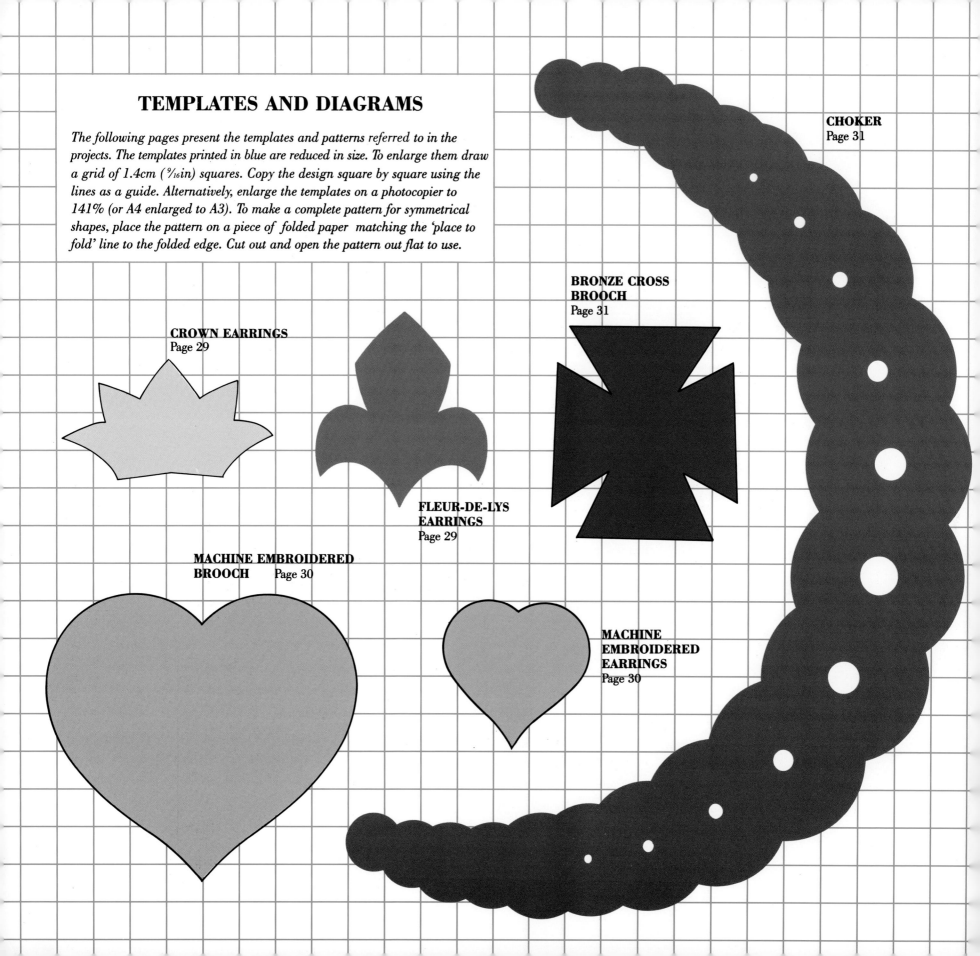

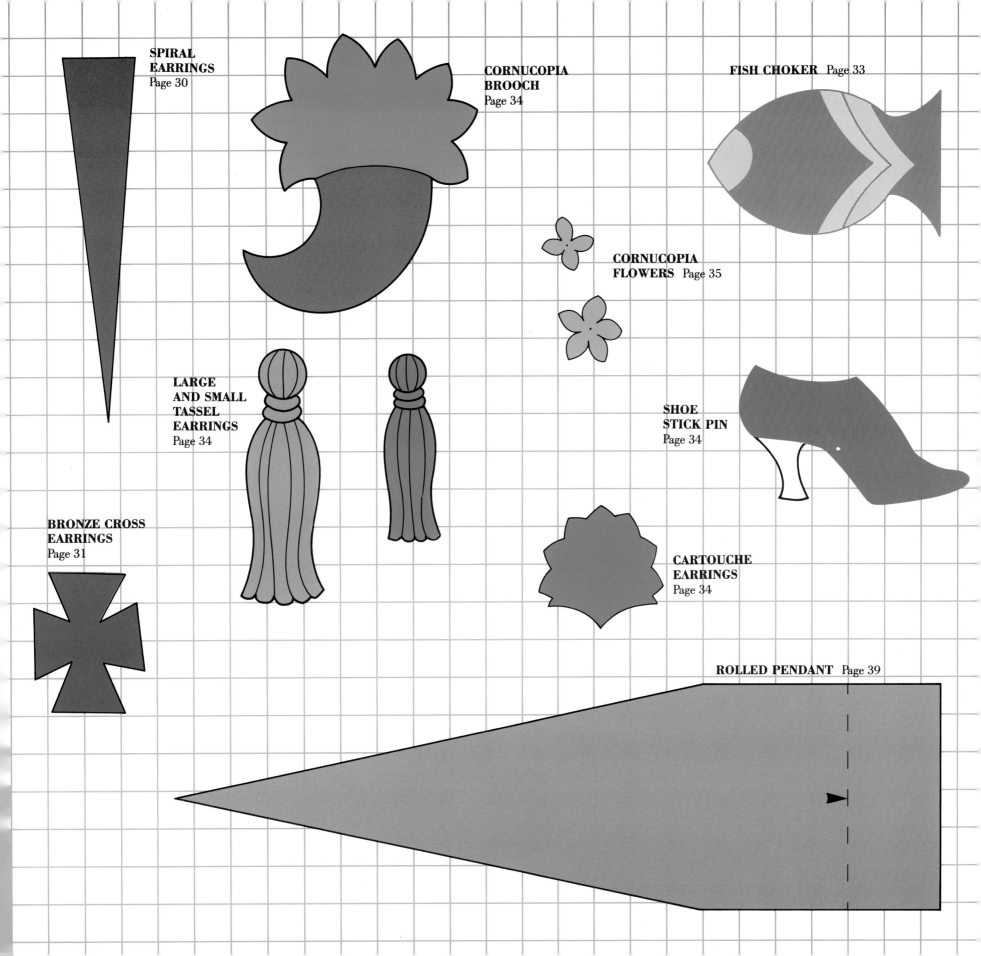

SPIRAL EARRINGS Page 30

CORNUCOPIA BROOCH Page 34

FISH CHOKER Page 33

CORNUCOPIA FLOWERS Page 35

LARGE AND SMALL TASSEL EARRINGS Page 34

SHOE STICK PIN Page 34

BRONZE CROSS EARRINGS Page 31

CARTOUCHE EARRINGS Page 34

ROLLED PENDANT Page 39

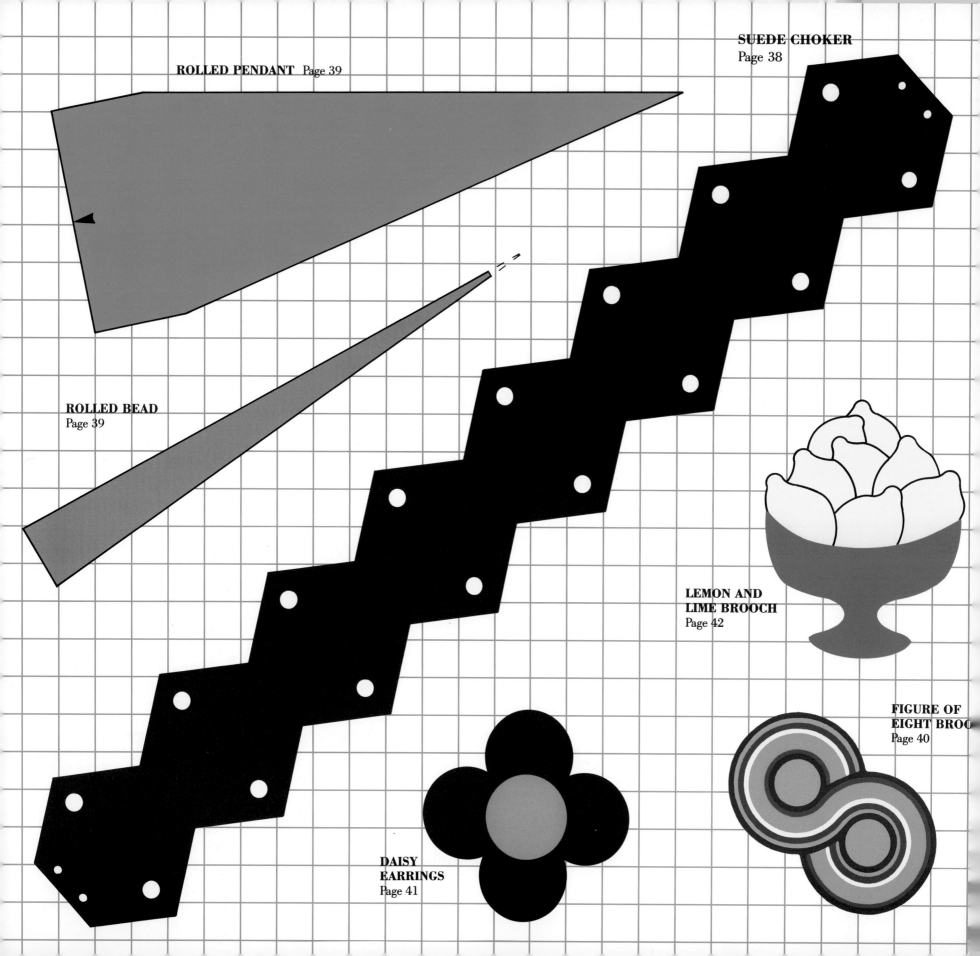

ROLLED PENDANT Page 39

SUEDE CHOKER
Page 38

ROLLED BEAD
Page 39

**LEMON AND
LIME BROOCH**
Page 42

**FIGURE OF
EIGHT BROO**
Page 40

**DAISY
EARRINGS**
Page 41

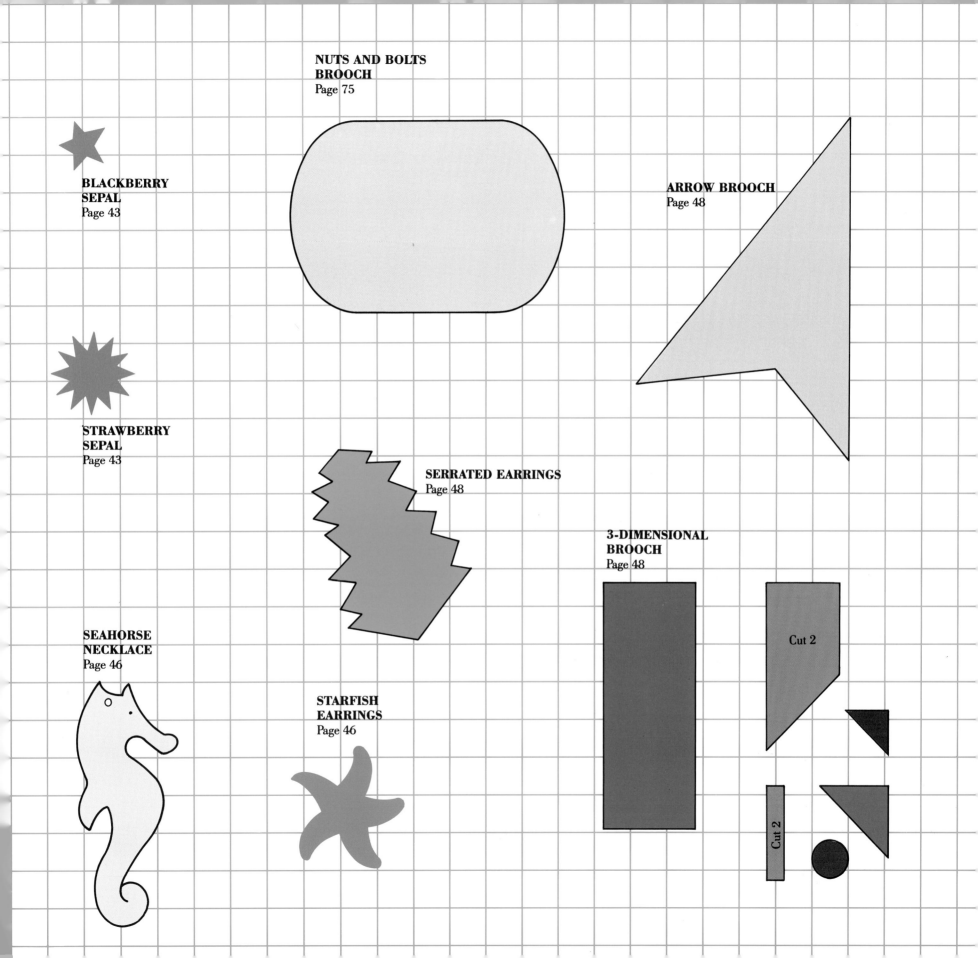

**NUTS AND BOLTS
BROOCH**
Page 75

**BLACKBERRY
SEPAL**
Page 43

ARROW BROOCH
Page 48

**STRAWBERRY
SEPAL**
Page 43

SERRATED EARRINGS
Page 48

**3-DIMENSIONAL
BROOCH**
Page 48

Cut 2

**SEAHORSE
NECKLACE**
Page 46

**STARFISH
EARRINGS**
Page 46

Cut 2

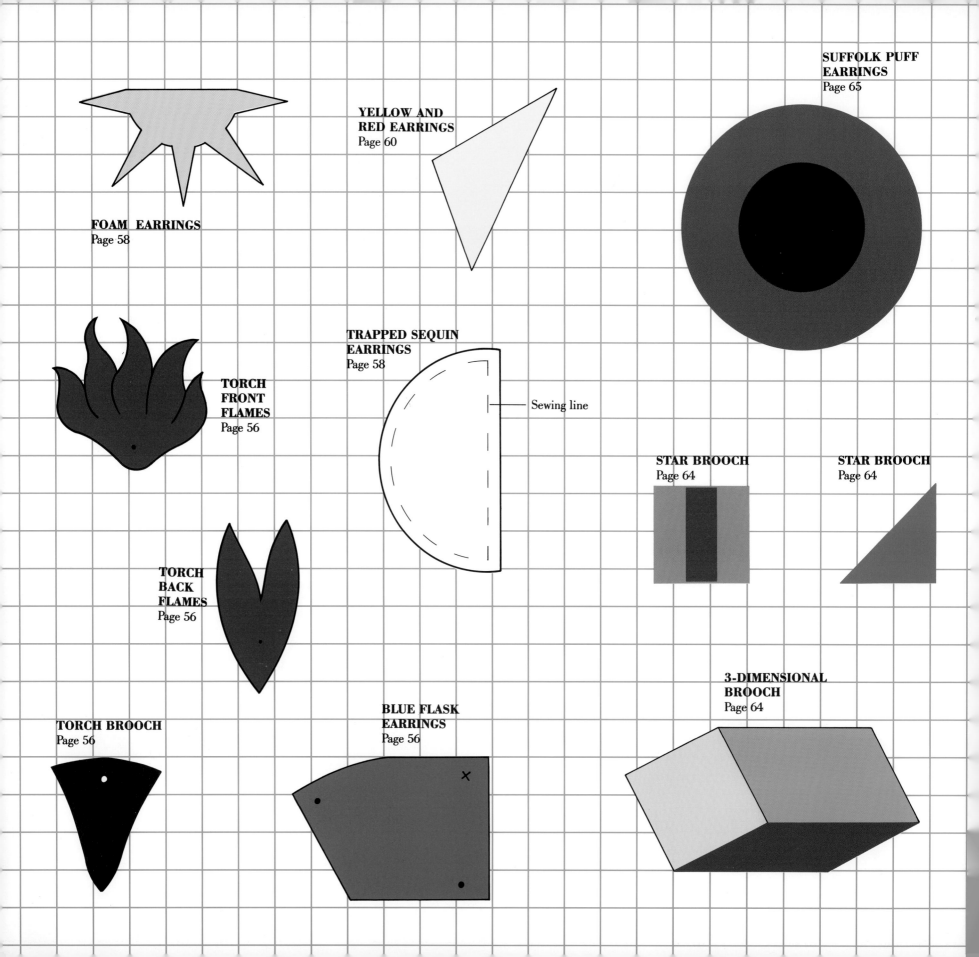

FOAM EARRINGS
Page 58

**YELLOW AND
RED EARRINGS**
Page 60

**SUFFOLK PUFF
EARRINGS**
Page 65

**TORCH
FRONT
FLAMES**
Page 56

**TRAPPED SEQUIN
EARRINGS**
Page 58

Sewing line

STAR BROOCH
Page 64

STAR BROOCH
Page 64

**TORCH
BACK
FLAMES**
Page 56

**3-DIMENSIONAL
BROOCH**
Page 64

TORCH BROOCH
Page 56

**BLUE FLASK
EARRINGS**
Page 56

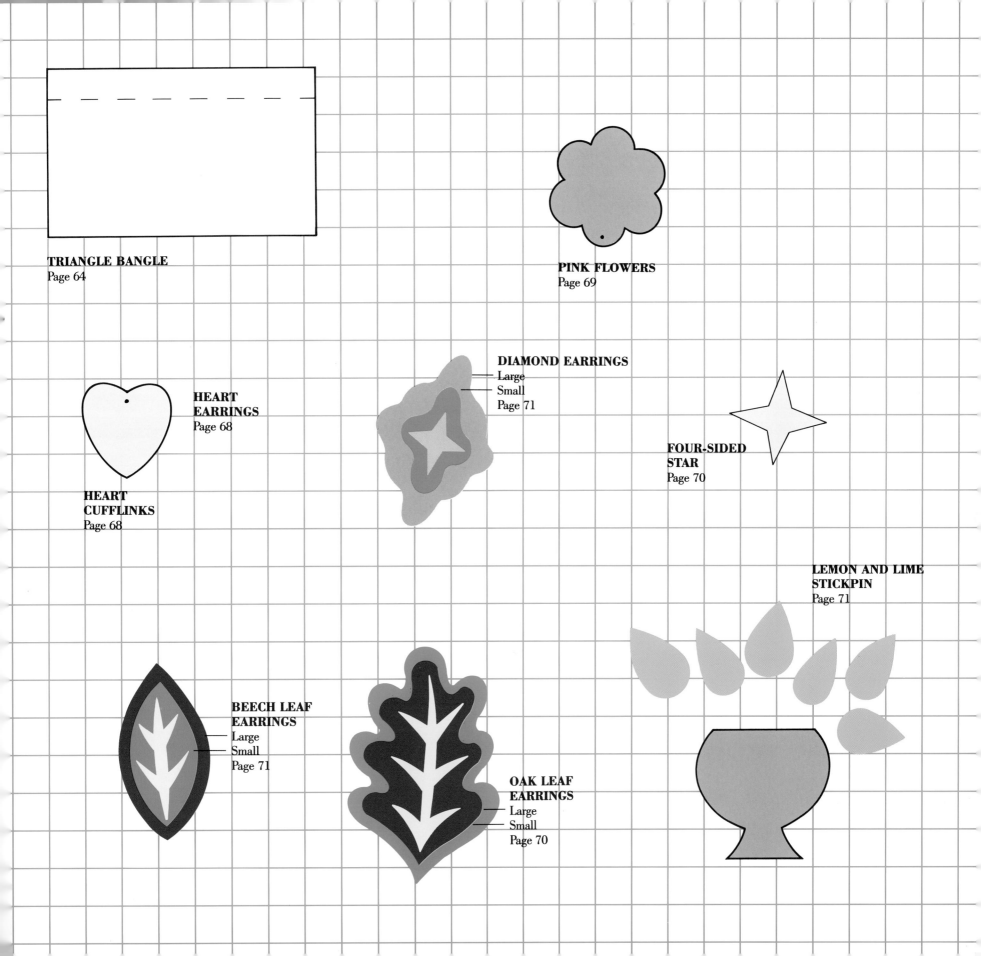

TRIANGLE BANGLE
Page 64

PINK FLOWERS
Page 69

**HEART
EARRINGS**
Page 68

**HEART
CUFFLINKS**
Page 68

DIAMOND EARRINGS
—Large
—Small
Page 71

**FOUR-SIDED
STAR**
Page 70

**LEMON AND LIME
STICKPIN**
Page 71

**BEECH LEAF
EARRINGS**
—Large
—Small
Page 71

**OAK LEAF
EARRINGS**
—Large
—Small
Page 70

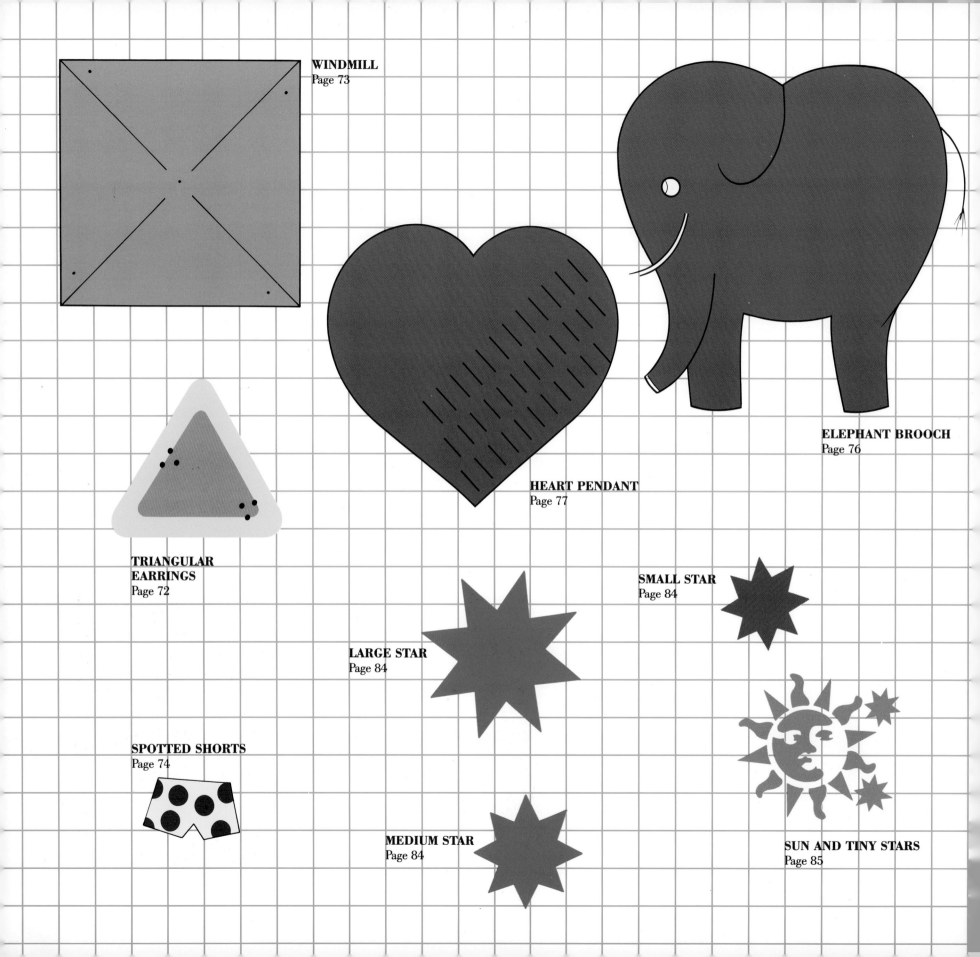

WINDMILL
Page 73

ELEPHANT BROOCH
Page 76

HEART PENDANT
Page 77

**TRIANGULAR
EARRINGS**
Page 72

SMALL STAR
Page 84

LARGE STAR
Page 84

SPOTTED SHORTS
Page 74

SUN AND TINY STARS
Page 85

MEDIUM STAR
Page 84

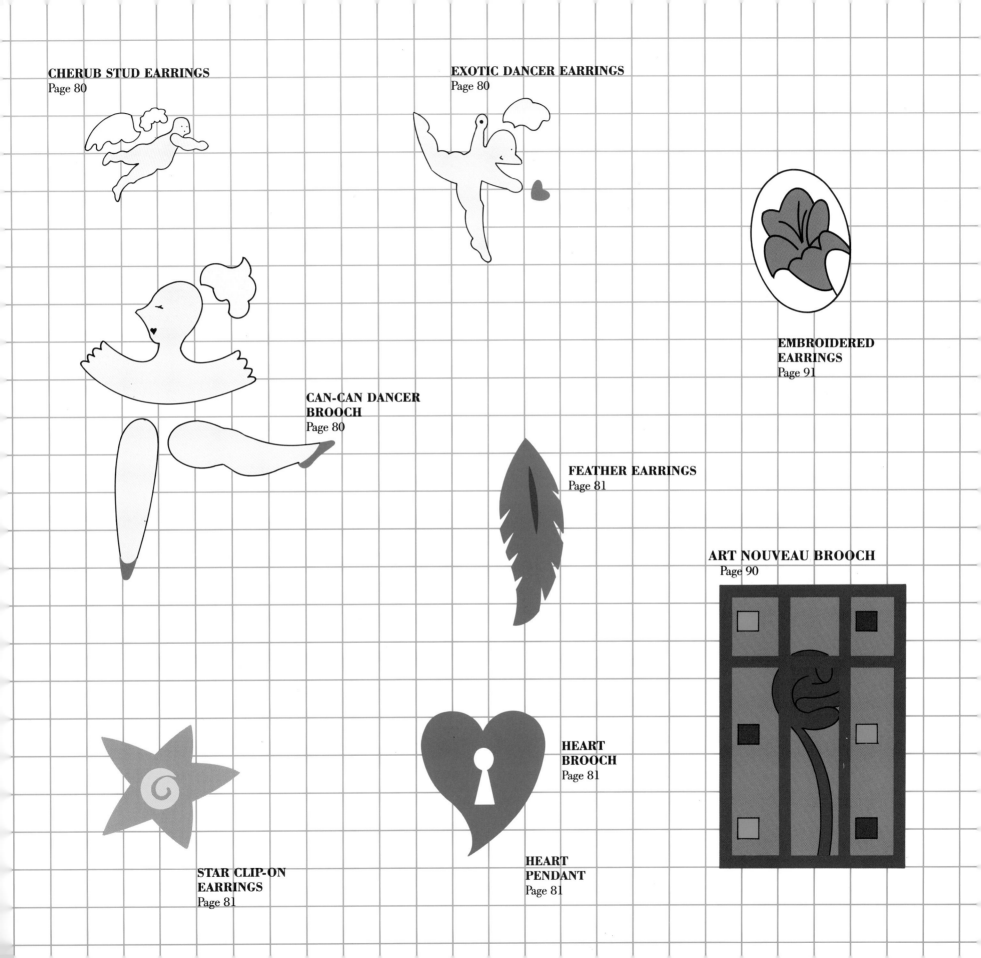

CHERUB STUD EARRINGS
Page 80

EXOTIC DANCER EARRINGS
Page 80

**EMBROIDERED
EARRINGS**
Page 91

**CAN-CAN DANCER
BROOCH**
Page 80

FEATHER EARRINGS
Page 81

ART NOUVEAU BROOCH
Page 90

**HEART
BROOCH**
Page 81

**STAR CLIP-ON
EARRINGS**
Page 81

**HEART
PENDANT**
Page 81

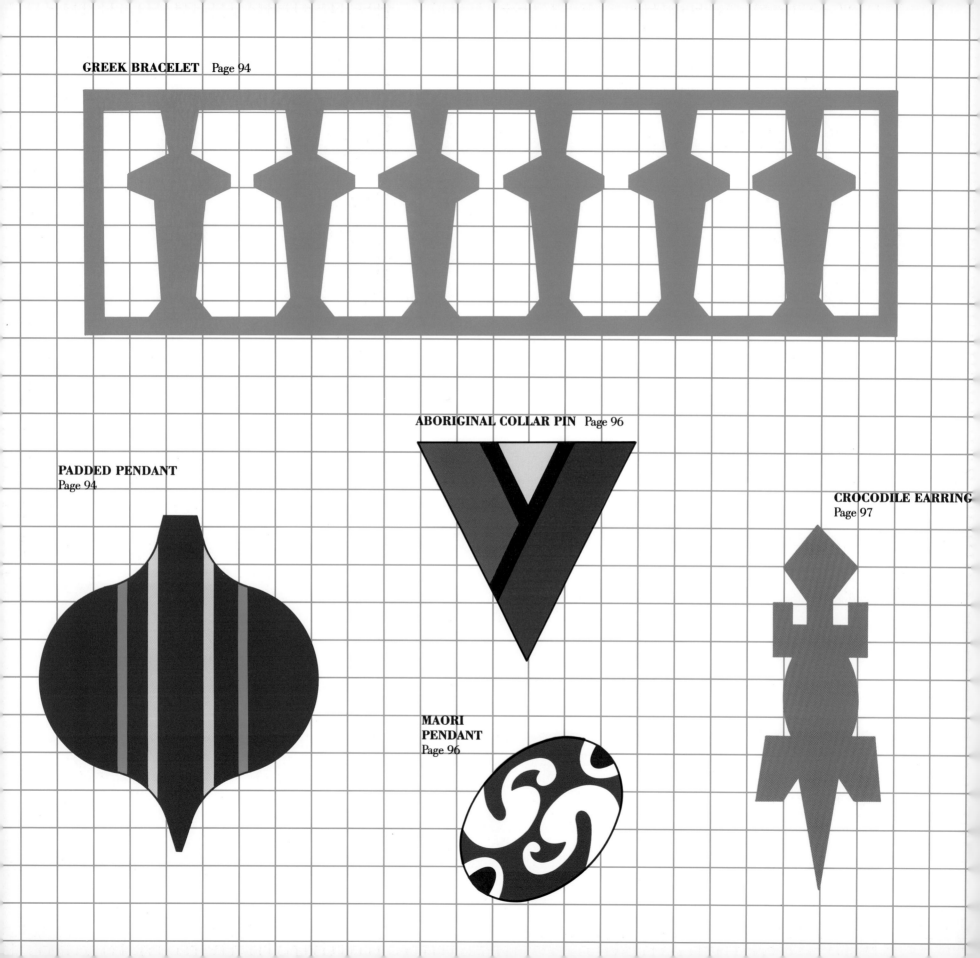

GREEK BRACELET Page 94

ABORIGINAL COLLAR PIN Page 96

PADDED PENDANT
Page 94

CROCODILE EARRING
Page 97

**MAORI
PENDANT**
Page 96

TURKISH EARRINGS

LOTUS BROOCH

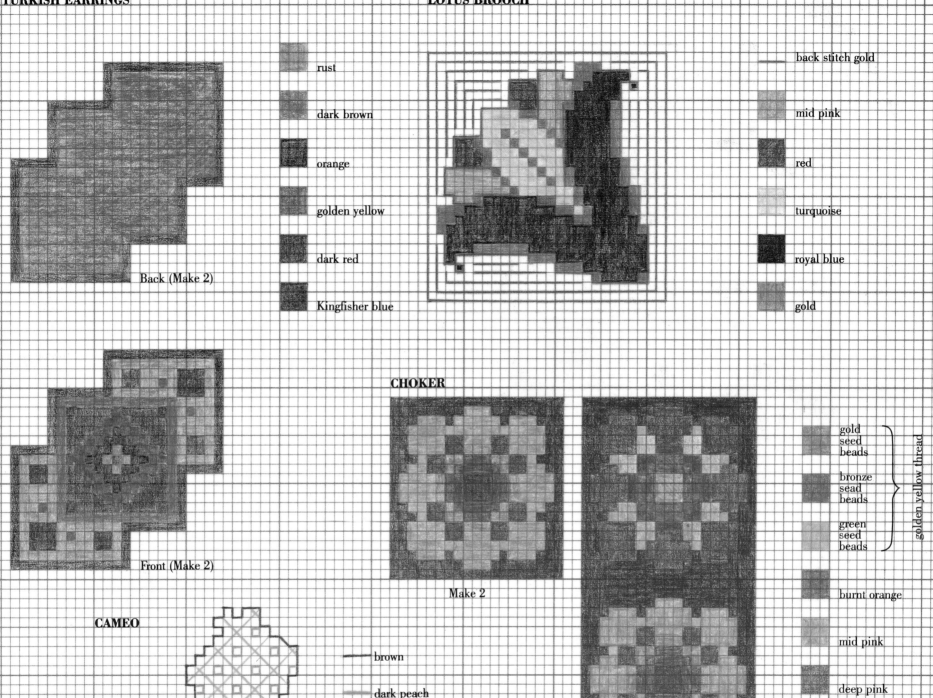

rust

dark brown

orange

golden yellow

dark red

Kingfisher blue

Back (Make 2)

back stitch gold

mid pink

red

turquoise

royal blue

gold

CHOKER

Front (Make 2)

Make 2

gold
seed
beads

bronze
sead
beads

green
seed
beads

golden yellow thread

burnt orange

mid pink

deep pink

burnt sienna

joining points

CAMEO

brown

dark peach

pink

Make 1

CREDITS

Managing Editor: Jo Finnis

Editor: Sue Wilkinson

Design: Phil Gorton

Photography: Steve Tanner

Photographic Direction: Nigel Duffield

Illustrations: Geoff Denney Associates

Typesetting: Mary Wray; Julie Smith

Production: Ruth Arthur; Sally Connolly; Neil Randles; Karen Staff; Jonathan Tickner

Production Director: Gerald Hughes

CONTRIBUTORS

Many thanks to the following for their help:
Alison Bruce for her work on pages 30-31, 62-63, 76-77, 92-93, 94-95, 96-97, 98-99.
Jan Eaton for her work on pages 92-93, 96-97, 98-99.
Jo Kaupe for the felt jewellery on pages 40-41.
Sandie Knudsen for the silk brooches on pages 32-33.
Pat Taylor for the patchwork bangle on pages 64-65.
Robert Claxton for all his help and advice throughout the making of this book.

ACKNOWLEDGEMENTS

Specialist yarns and purl-beads from Barnyarns Ltd, Dept DM3, Langrish, Petersfield,
Hants. GU32 1RQ. Tel 01730 233010
Sewing machine for photographs from Bernina Sewing Machines, 50-52 Great Sutton Street,
London EC1V 0DJ. Tel 0171 253 1198
Embroidery yarns from Coats Patons Crafts PO Box, McMullen Road, Darlington, Co Durham. DL1 1YQ. Tel 01325 381010
Beads, findings and other items from Janet Coles Beads Ltd, 128 Notting Hill Gate,
London W11 3QG. Tel 0171 727 8085
Stranded cotton from DMC Creative World Ltd, Pullman Road, Wigston, Leicestershire LE18 2DY. Tel 01533 811040
Brooch frames from Framecraft Miniatures Ltd, 372-376 Summer Lane, Hockley,
Birmingham B19 3QA. Tel 0121 212 0551
Craft materials from Inscribe Ltd, Woolmer Industrial Estate, Bordon, Hampshire GU35 9QE. Tel 01420 475747
Iron on dots and some frames from Lofoten Designs 486 St Vincent Street,
Glasgow G3 8XU. Tel 0141 204 1056
Craft materials from Maple Textiles 188-190 Maple Road, London SE20 8HT. Tel 0181 778 8049
Leather from A. L. Maugham & Co Ltd, 5 Fazakerley Street,
Liverpool L3 9DN.Tel 0151 236 1872
Ribbons from C. M. Offray & Son Ltd, Fir Tree Place, Church Road, Ashford, Middlesex TW15 2PH. Tel 01784 247281
Gloving leather from Pittards Plc, Sherborne Road, Yeovil,
Somerset BA21 5BA. Tel 01935 74321
Craft products from Panduro Hobby, Westway Ho, Transport Avenue, Brentford, Middlesex TW8 9HF. Tel 0181 847 6161
Quilting materials from Quilt Basics, Dept TQ, 2 Meads Lane, Chesham,
Bucks. HP5 1ND. Tel 01494 785202
Embroidery threads from Silken Strands, 33 Linksway, Gatley, Cheshire SK8 4LA. Tel 01614 289108
Silk paints and materials from George Weil and Sons Ltd, 18 Hanson Street,
London W1P 7DB. Tel 0171 580 3763
Photographic properties from Nice Irma's Ltd, 46 Goodge Street, London W1P 1FJ. Tel 0171 580 6921
Photographic properties from John Lewis Plc, 278-306 Oxford Street, London W1A 1EX. Tel 0171 629 7711